THE

CW01025346

BASINGSTOKE

RIOTS

MASSAGAINIANS v THE SALVATION ARMY

1880-1883

by

Bob Clarke

Bob Clarke

22 October 2010

BASINGSTOKE ARCHAEOLOGICAL & HISTORICAL SOCIETY

BAHSOC

by the same author

From Grub Street to Fleet Street:
An Illustrated History of English
Newspapers to 1899

© Bob Clarke 2010

Published by the Basingstoke Archaeological & Historical Society
(charity no 1000263)

www.bahsoc.org.uk

First published 2010

A CIP data record for this title is available from the British Library.

ISBN 978–0–9508095–6–4

Line drawings by Alan Turton

Typesetting and design by Palindrome

Printed and bound by Wyeth Ltd of Alton

CONTENTS

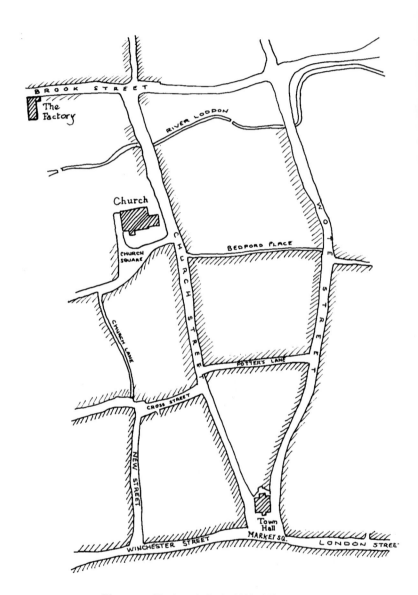

The centre of Basingstoke in the 1880s (Alan Turton)

ACKNOWLEDGEMENTS

I would like to thank the staff of Basingstoke Library for their patience in loading the microfilm reader on about fifty occasions for me because I was too lazy and incompetent to learn how to do it myself. Without their help I would not have been able to quote from the back copies of the *Hants and Berks Gazette*. I am also grateful to the staffs at the National Archives and the Hampshire Record Office for digging out files and other material that proved invaluable in providing a rounded picture of events in early 1880s Basingstoke.

I am particularly grateful to John Hollands and Sue Tapliss at the Willis Museum. To John for delaying his lunch on several occasions to find and photocopy piles of documents for me from the Local Studies Room, including the *Report of the Proceedings before the Magistrates, on May 3rd and 9th, 1881* and the transcriptions George Woodman made of his diaries in 1928 and 1930; and to Sue for giving up so much time to hunt out and download photographs (Hampshire County Council Museums & Arts Service) to be used in the book.

Grateful thanks also to:

- Jean Halton, archivist of the London Street United Reformed Church for letting me have a photocopy of the Arthur Hailstone manuscript and for arranging for us to photograph the picture of Henry Barron;
- Debbie Collins, Mayoral Coordinator, for the pictures of Richard and Arthur Wallis and John Burgess Soper (by courtesy of the Borough of Basingstoke and Deane);
- Jean Willoughby, Albert Lansley's granddaughter for permission to use the photograph of Albert;
- Robert Brown for the use of two photographs;
- Alan Turton for the map and line drawings;
- Mark Jones, editor of the *Basingstoke Gazette* for permission to use extracts from its predecessor, the *Hants & Berks Gazette*, and Richard Garfield for finding the drawing of John Bird, its founder and first editor;.
- Paula Turner for her design skills.

Special thanks are due to Bob and Barbara Applin for giving up a considerable amount of their time, whole days on many occasions, to provide advice and editorial comments. I was reliant on Bob's photographic skills and on Barbara's eagle eye to spot and tone down some of my more infelicitous remarks in the earlier drafts of the text. Without their help, and the backing of the Basingstoke Archaeological & Historical Society, in particular the work of its Publications Sub-Committee, this book would not have been published.

Finally, I would like to thank the Massagainians, whose antics 130 years ago kept me amused during the months I was researching this book.

Two 'Hallelujah Lasses' (Courtesy of The Salvation Army) and Two Massagainians (Alan Turton)

BEER AND BASINGSTOKE

About midway between London and Salisbury there is a benighted little town
which appears to be inhabited chiefly by a race of barbarians . . . Can nothing be
done for Barbarous Basingstoke? Cannot the Church Missionary Society open
a special fund to send a missionary to bring this dark spot within the pale of
Christian civilisation?

The [London evening] Echo, 15 March 1882

Basingstoke is notorious for two events: burying the same woman alive
twice, and the Salvation Army riots of 1881. In 1674 the town buried a
Mrs Blunden, believing she was dead. But they dug her up again after
some children playing in the graveyard told an adult that they had heard
'fearful Groans and dismal Shriekings' and cries of 'Take me out of my
grave' coming from below. They found her body 'lamentably beaten' in a
frenzied attempt to escape from her coffin. Thinking she was finally dead,
they buried her again. When the coroner ordered the body to be exhumed
some days later, they found that she had moved after they had buried her
the second time. She had since torn off her winding sheet, there were more
scratches, and she had 'beaten her Mouth so long till it was all in gore
Blood'.[1]

But it was the Salvation Army riots that really put Basingstoke on the
map. The riots were reported in the national press, gave rise to questions in
the House of Commons and even led to the publication of a parliamentary
paper, *Basingstoke Disturbances: Return containing copies of any correspondence
which has been passed between the Home Office and the Local Authorities of
Basingstoke, or other places, with reference to the Suppression of Disturbances*.[2]

As recently as 1998 the Basingstoke riots were still being mentioned
in Parliament. During a House of Commons debate about banning
Orangemen from parading through Nationalist areas in Northern Ireland
for fear that they would provoke violent counter-demonstrations, William
Ross, the Ulster Unionist MP, suggested that the counter-demonstrations
were orchestrated by the IRA. He referred back to the Basingstoke riots.
He compared the Mayor and publicans of Basingstoke to the IRA. ('All one

---

1 *News from/BASING-STOAK/Of one/Mrs BLUNDEN/A Maltsters Wife, who
was/Buried Alive.* n.d (1674?).
2 Parliamentary Papers (1882) Cmd, 132, vol. 54.

has to do is take away "Mayor Blatch" and the "liquor interests" and insert "IRA" . . . and one has the exact same set-up that we have seen in recent years in Northern Ireland.')[3]

It was reported from a number of different eye witnesses that 3,000 people took to the streets during one of the riots – not bad for town with a population of only 6,681.[4] Not all of those 3,000 lived in the town – there are references to lads coming in from the villages to join in the fun. And not all of them were rioters – some would have been Salvationists and their supporters and some were spectators. Reports indicate that there was a hard core of some 200 who were physically involved in disrupting the Salvation Army – the self-styled Massagainians. Unfortunately we only know the names of the small minority who appeared before the borough magistrates. Biographical notes about some of those characters and certain other players are in Appendix 1. It is clear that many other people in the town, who did not take part in the disturbances, sympathised with the Massagainians.

The arrival of the Salvation Army opened a rift between church and chapel. Rival petitions signed by over a thousand Basingstoke townsfolk showed that the town was split in two between those who supported the Salvation Army, and those who were against it. Even the town's magistrates and councillors were bitterly divided on the issue.

Nowadays we regard the Salvation Army as being a rather benign organisation, doing lots of useful social work amongst the poor both here and abroad; enhancing the spirit of Christmas with their brass bands playing carols in town centres; and providing comfort to those who are looking for a better life in the hereafter. But in the early 1880s many Basingstoke people regarded the Salvation Army with hostility and, in some cases, with fear. If the main purpose of the Salvation Army was saving souls, its secondary, and high-profile, purpose in the early 1880s was clamping down on the demon drink.

The Salvation Army began life as the Christian Mission, founded by William and Catherine Booth in 1865. In 1878, Booth decided that the movement would be more effective if it was organised on military lines, with a clear chain of command reporting to him, as General. Each corps, covering a town, was headed by a captain, usually assisted by a lieutenant. Corps were arranged into districts, under the command of a major; and several districts formed a division commanded by a colonel.

The Army's uniforms were intended to appeal to jingoism among the Victorian working classes. Its military language reflected its mission to wage war against sin. Its prayer meetings were called Knee Drill and its tracts were called Hallelujah Torpedoes. (The Admiralty started production of

---

3   House of Commons Debates, 4 Feb 1998 col. 1109.
4   1881 census.

torpedoes in 1872. They were the Navy's latest weapon, so the word had a special resonance.)

The Salvation Army was in the business of conversion. It was not good enough simply to hold your services inside your own building. You had to go outside to where the sinners congregated if you stood any chance of saving their souls; hence the emphasis on colourful and noisy processions that would attract the crowds, and hymn singing and prayer meetings outside pubs and in the Market Place where people usually gathered. Through its open-air ministry, the Salvation Army reached the parts of the working class other denominations could not reach.

It was the Army's open-air ministry that alienated a considerable portion of 'respectable', middle-class opinion in the town. Those who didn't go to church were annoyed by the Sunday morning processions disturbing the peace and quiet of what was supposed to be their day of rest. Secular Basingstoke did not want street preachers shouting ejaculations and ramming religion down their throats at ten o'clock on a Sunday morning or on weekday evenings.

Additionally, the clergy and churchgoers were offended by the use of daily familiar language to defile what they considered to be sacred, and they regarded the Army's use of popular music-hall tunes for some of their hymns as blasphemous. Church of England clergy, with one or two exceptions, took a rather snobbish attitude towards the Salvation Army in its early days. They considered the uneducated and unordained evangelists to be notoriety seekers unqualified to preach, and that they were guilty of promulgating an unsound theology. Also, as is well known, the Church of England had a massive prejudice against women preachers. Many in the Church of England, and many non-churchgoers who regarded religion as being a private matter, saw the Salvation Army as coarse and irreverent, serving only to bring religion into disrepute.

By contrast, the non-conformist sects welcomed the arrival of the Salvation Army. They admired its crusading zeal, and felt that the spirit of Wesley and Whitfield had returned in the form of the Army to usher in a new age of working class evangelism.

Booth's early years as an independent street preacher in London's East End had convinced him, probably with justification in some extreme cases, that drink was the single most critical factor responsible for the moral degradation of the population. Public houses were the repository of sin. Only by giving up the drink could one achieve salvation.

Beer was important to the people of Basingstoke. There were some 50 pubs and beer houses in the town (see Appendix 2). Their warmth, comfort, companionship, conviviality and good cheer at the end of a hard day's work was a welcome alternative to cold, ill-lit, and often overcrowded homes. Basingstoke also hosted four breweries: the Victoria Brewery run

May's Brewery, c. 1860 (Hampshire County Council Museums & Arts Service)

by the Adams family; Barrett's Flaxfield Road brewery; the Wote Street brewery, which Barretts had recently purchased from Frederick Blunden; and May's enormous brewery in Brook Street. These breweries employed large numbers of townsfolk. Many people in ancillary trades also depended on the pubs and breweries for their living, in addition to the 50 landlords and landladies and their families. Running a pub was a precarious business. Many publicans had to have other jobs on the side in order to feed their families. Taking the *Cattle Market Tavern* (now the *Bounty*) as an example, William Sayer, the landlord to 1880, was also the local gunsmith. His successor, James Strong, doubled as a boot repairer. James Heath, who took over the licence in 1882, also worked as a painter and glazier. Finding work at that time was not easy. The Great Agricultural Depression and increasing mechanisation caused a severe reduction in the numbers of farm workers. People were leaving the villages and moving to towns like Basingstoke in search of work.

Basingstoke people could well imagine that their way of life, and in many cases their livelihood, was under threat. As well as the various temperance societies that flourished in mid-Victorian Britain, there was an influential prohibitionist movement, the United Kingdom Alliance, which was formed in 1853 to campaign for the 'Suppression of the Traffic in all Intoxicating Liquors'. The Alliance was inspired by the American Maine

The banner for the local newspaper, where many of the incidents in this story were reported in detail.

Law that was passed in 1851 to establish prohibition throughout the state of Maine. It wanted to close down all the pubs and breweries in this country. Manufacturers and other businessmen put up the money to support the Alliance, as they believed prohibition would benefit them financially. Sober workmen would be more disciplined and productive. They wouldn't keep taking Mondays off to nurse their hangovers. Once they stopped spending their money on drink, they could spend it on consumer goods and boost the businessmen's profits.

The Alliance attracted support from the temperance societies and the nonconformist churches. It also attracted killjoys. Alliance members warned parliamentary candidates that they would withhold their votes unless the candidates promised to vote for prohibition. They managed to infiltrate Liberal constituency associations to select candidates who were sympathetic to their cause. The Alliance's supporters in Parliament recognised that countrywide prohibition could not be introduced overnight, so MPs like Sir Wilfred Lawson and W. S. Caine introduced a number of Bills that would allow local authorities to declare their areas dry, following the Maine precedent. By this step by step approach they hoped eventually to turn the whole country dry. In June 1880 the House of Commons passed a Local Option Resolution by 245 votes to 219. As it happened, it never became law. The government had more pressing matters to contend with, not least the matter of Home Rule for Ireland. But the brewers and publicans of Basingstoke were not to know that. During the early 1880s there was a very real concern that Parliament would introduce prohibition.

That concern was heightened by the prominence given to abstinence campaigners in the pages of the *Hants and Berks Gazette*. John Bird, the proprietor of the *Gazette*, was a member of the Basingstoke Total Abstinence Society. As far as I can be sure, he had three reporters covering events in the town at the time of the disturbances: his teenage brother, Sydney; Alfred Taplin, who was also the organist at the London Street Congregational Church; and William Thompson, who was to be a prosecution witness in a case brought by the Salvation Army against the rioters. During that case, Thompson described himself as being 'not a member of the Salvation Army, but I sympathise with their rights'.

Later, in 1881, he was presented with an expensive travelling bag and an illuminated address by the Directors of the Old Angel Café, 'in recognition of his indefatigable labours in the cause of Temperance, and a testimony to the fearless and conscientious manner in which he discharged the duties of a reporter during an important epoch in the history of the town'.[5] Together they ensured that the frequent meetings of the various teetotal societies in Basingstoke got the fullest coverage.

Other prominent supporters of war against drink included Thomas Burberry, the clothing manufacturer, who was President of the Basingstoke Total Abstinence Society; Rev. Henry Barron, Minister of the London Street Congregational Church; Richard Wallis, the Senior Magistrate; Alderman Arthur Wallis of Wallis and Steevens; and Councillors John Burgess Soper, Thomas Maton Kingdon, President of the local branch of the teetotal Blue Ribbon Army, and Arkas Sapp, who was a deacon at the London Street Congregational Church.

The Basingstoke Total Abstinence Society used to invite officials from the Alliance to speak at their meetings. In July 1882 Basingstoke hosted a Great County Demonstration in favour of Local Option whose speakers included the MP, Sir Wilfred Lawson. Lawson told his Basingstoke audience that drunkenness brought upon us a greater calamity than the combined evils of war, pestilence and famine; that the Alliance's aim was to stop the trade in beer; and, in answer to the claim that this would ruin the poor publicans, he gave the heartless advice, 'Let them sell groceries, or boots, or anything to gain an honest living.'[6]

If the Alliance represented the constitutional arm of the prohibitionist movement, the Salvation Army was perceived by many as being its paramilitary arm. Here was a uniformed body, with their military ranks and discipline, marching round the town four abreast crying 'Ban all drink!', their flag emblazoned with the motto 'Blood and Fire'. They held open air meetings that began with a call for repentance and ended with a plea for total abstinence, and occasionally they gathered outside pubs calling on the customers to give up the booze. In Ipswich the Salvation Army used to stand outside pubs shouting, 'Come out of the Devil's House!'[7] It is possible that the Army in Basingstoke was doing something similar. Their objective was quite clear, to quote Catherine Booth when she visited Basingstoke:

> What we are trying to do . . . is to try to invent some new measure
> – some aggressive means of drawing those debauched classes out of
> the public houses, of letting them know they are going to hell.[8]

5   *Hants and Berks Gazette*, 16 July 1881.
6   *Hants and Berks Gazette*, 14 July 1882.
7   *Ipswich Journal*, 1 July 1884.
8   Clements, Ken, *Two Feeble Women: The Early History of the Salvation Army in*

General Booth, in a memorandum of 23 March 1881 to Sir William Harcourt, the Home Secretary, said,

> We commenced in Basingstoke in October last, and the meetings, both in the streets and in our own buildings, have been carried on with great success, hundreds of men and women having been reclaimed from lives of open sin . . . of course, the trade of the Publicans and Brewers has suffered very much. They are correspondingly infuriated against us.[9]

It is little wonder that many people wanted to drive the Salvation Army out of Basingstoke. The Army was seen as threatening their way of life, and in many cases, their means of earning a living. They could not lash out at the Alliance and its parliamentary supporters, but the Salvation Army was a handy target. One motivation for the attacks was that the attackers were reclaiming the streets and defending their right to drink against a bunch of uniformed invaders, who wanted to close down the pubs and drive the publicans and brewery employees out of work.

Another motivation for the attacks was resentment felt by these pioneers of Basingstoke yobbery at renegades from their own class denouncing them as sinners for enjoying their beer, and calling on them to repent. This was a natural hostility to self-righteous 'respectability'. The resentment grew more intense after the Salvation Army began private prosecutions against those who had been disrupting their services. However, I suspect the main motivation for disrupting the Salvation Army's meetings was because it was great fun, and there was free beer in it. For the Basingstoke binge drinkers of 1881, the riots were probably the most exciting thing they had ever enjoyed. In an era deficient in public amusements, they were a way of letting off steam. Some people nowadays moan that there is nothing to do in Basingstoke. There was even less in 1881.

The story of the Salvation Army riots is the story of the clash of two competing rights. One was the right to drink and, for many, the right to continue to earn a living at the brewery or from running a pub. The other was the right to hold processions and open air meetings. Both parties considered that their liberties were the birthright of every English man and woman. The first was sanctified by tradition; the other was hard fought for over the preceding centuries in the struggles for political and religious freedom.

Basingstoke (no publisher noted, *c*. 1995).
9   TNA PRO HO 45/9607/A2886 *Disturbances: Salvation Army Meetings and Processions in Basingstoke.*

BASINGSTOKE IN 1881

Basingstoke is a straggling, ill-built town, situated to the left in the valley . . . The inhabitants now mainly depend on the corn and malt trades.

Bradshaw's Illustrated Handbook for Tourists (1881)

In 1881, the borough of Basingstoke covered some 4,000 acres stretching from Oakridge in the north to Kempshott in the south and from Deadman's Lane in the east to Roman Road on the west. Most of the borough was farmland or meadows. Apart from a small settlement at Worting Town's End, most people lived in the town within the rectangle of some 200 acres formed by the railway to the north, Southern Road to the south, Eastrop Lane to the east and Essex Road to the west. Everything else was open country. And even within the town there was farmland and meadows. The river Loddon ran through the town, and there were several brooks and streams meandering through the meadows between Essex Road and St Michael's Church. In the rainy seasons, one of the streams used to flood the houses at the bottom of Flaxfield Road.

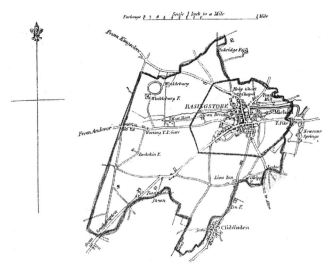

This map, taken from the Boundary Commissioners' report for Basingstoke in 1837, showed the existing borough boundary (the outer line) and the proposed reduced area (the inner line) which was never approved. In 1881 the outer line was still the boundary.

For centuries Basingstoke has existed mainly as a market town for the surrounding countryside. But, with the decline in agriculture, Basingstoke was beginning to find new life as a manufacturing centre with Wallis and Steevens' iron foundry and Gerrish, Ames and Simpkins' clothing factory dominating both sides of Station Hill. Other major employers included the London and South Western and Great Western railway companies, May's Brewery, and Burberry's and Mares' clothing companies.

As a result, the population within the borough had grown from 5,574 to 6,691 in the ten years since 1871, and was to grow still further to 7,960 by 1891. To accommodate the increased population, there was a great deal of building work going on. There had already been a marked increase in the number of houses in the borough – from 1,162 in 1871 to 1,460 in 1881 – and the town was still expanding, mainly terraces of red brick and slate cottages in Newtown along the valley between Worting Road and the railway, and in the Essex Road area, built by Mr Tyrrell, who came from Essex and named the streets after towns in his home county.

Workers' cottages were generally rented out for between £10 and £12 a year. There is an advertisement in the *Hants and Berks Gazette* for a cottage to let in Longcroft Road, Newtown (later May Street), 'Rent 4s 6d a week, rates included, water laid on.' Many people subsidised their rent bills by taking in lodgers, usually for 2s 6d a week. Further up the scale, the *Gazette* advertised 4 Sarum Villas to let, 'containing dining and drawing rooms, kitchen, four bedrooms, large cellar and usual offices, and servant's attic – Rent £25 a year.'[10] To get to today's (retail) prices, you would need to multiply 1881 prices by at least 60. The multiplier for wage inflation would be much higher. Men working in manual trades were generally paid less than £1 a week.

In the commercial streets of the town – London Street, Winchester Street, Wote Street and Church Street – there was a mixture of shops, pubs and private houses. Many of the shopkeepers lived with their families above their shops, often with their staff. The 1881 census shows that, on the night of Sunday, 3 April, the following were living in Arkas Sapp's chemist's shop in the Market Place, on the corner of Wote Street and London Street:

Arkas Sapp	Head	34	Chemist, druggist and grocer
Sarah A Sapp	Wife	34	
Marguerita Sapp	Daughter	3	
Alice Sapp	Daughter	1	
John Sapp	Son	0	
George Woodman	Servant	36	Chemist, druggist assistant
Ellen Mallard	Servant	16	Nurse domestic
Eliza Nickless	Servant	19	General servant

10   *Hants and Berks Gazette*, 12 February 1881.

The billhead for Arkas Sapp, chemist, shows his shop on the corner of London Street and the Market Place. (Hampshire County Council Museums & Arts Service)

Although the railway had destroyed the coaching trade, and badly affected the coaching inns that had given so much employment to Basingstoke people, there was still a need to transport goods between Basingstoke and the outlying towns and villages that were not on the railway. Carriers left the *Feathers* for Baughurst, Kingsclere, Odiham, Pamber, Ramsdell, Sherfield on Loddon, Tadley, Weston Patrick, Whitchurch and Woodmancote on Wednesdays. A carrier left the *Engineers' Arms* for Alton on Tuesdays and Saturdays and for Newbury on Thursdays and Mondays, while one left the *Angel* on Wednesdays for Hartley Wespall and another left the *Angel* for Preston Candover on Wednesdays and Saturdays; North Waltham received a daily service from the *Three Tuns* and a Wednesday service from the *Rose and Crown*; Overton also enjoyed a daily service from a carrier from the *Harrow*; while Sherfield on Loddon and Tadley, which received their Wednesday service from the *Feathers*, were also served from the *Railway Arms* and the *Self Defence* respectively. Again, this shows the importance of the public houses in the lives of the community. In addition, coroners' inquests were held in pubs. When a tailor cut his own throat in the *Cattle Market* in July 1881, the inquest was held in the *Rising Sun*.

Most people could not afford to own their own horses, and, until the invention of the mass-produced safety bicycle, penny-farthing bicycles and the newly-invented large-wheeled tricycle were way beyond the means of all but the very rich. Unless one could afford the train fare (assuming where you wanted to go was served by the railway) or could hitch a ride from a carrier, the only means of transport was by foot. On the night of Saturday 28 May 1881 there was trouble at the *Royal Exchange* public house. One of those accused of being drunk was a lad called Marlow who was asleep in the bar. It later transpired that it wasn't excess beer that made him sleepy, but the fact that he had walked from Oxford that day.

Religion played a large part in Victorian life, and we are told that church and chapel attendance was high. The religious census of those attending services at the various places of worship in the borough on Sunday 12 February 1882 produced the following:

St Michael's Church	1,073
St Mary's, Eastrop	169
London Street Congregational Church	743
New Road Congregational Chapel	59
Worting Town's End Congregational Chapel	72
Countess of Huntingdon's Connexion, Wote Street	291
Wesleyan Chapel, Church Street	257
Roman Catholic Church, Burgess Road	112
Baptist Church, Church Street	155
Salvation Army, Brook Street	586
Quakers, Wote Street	22
Plymouth Brethren and other Nonconformists	339

The total of 3,878 seems high for a population of 6,681. However, there is likely to be a considerable element of double counting, as the figures represent the total attendance at both morning and evening services, and many people would have attended both. Also, there are likely to have been people attending from the villages and farms outside the borough.

LAW AND ORDER

Basingstoke had two Police Stations: the County Police Station in Mark Lane, which was responsible for policing outside the Borough; and the Borough Police Station situated on the east side of New Street. New Street Police Station, built in 1816, also served as the Superintendent's home and the town gaol. The Borough police force comprised Superintendent Mark Hibberd, Sergeant Waldren and five constables (Hurst, Mears, Simpson, Trodd and Astridge in 1881) until it was amalgamated with the County Force in 1889. If the magistrates wanted to augment the Borough Police for any special occasion by borrowing members of the County Police, the town's ratepayers would have to pay the County for the privilege. Therefore, there was generally a reluctance to bring in the County force.

Borough policemen, 1889.
From left to right, back row: Sergeant William Trodd and Constables William Mears,
William Astridge, Charles Treagus. Front row: Constables James White, Clement Burden,
James Hibberd. (Hampshire County Council Museums & Arts Service)

At the beginning of 1881 the Borough magistrates, otherwise known as the Basingstoke Petty Court, were the Mayor, William Blatch, as Chief Magistrate; the ex-Mayor, Alderman Henry Allen; Richard Wallis, the Senior Magistrate; Richard Knight; Alderman Arthur Wallis; and Alderman Henry Portsmouth. They met, usually once a week on Tuesdays, to hear cases brought before them by the Borough Police and private individuals.

Apart from cases connected with the Salvation Army, the cases brought before the magistrates during the period 1881 to 1883 provide a vivid picture of the underside of Basingstoke life. Cases included vagrancy, bastardy, larceny, being drunk and disorderly, or drunk and incapable, refusing to leave licensed premises when requested, arson, assault (including one case where the defendant was the gloriously named Goliath Cole), attempting to commit suicide, malicious damage, cruelty to horses, illegal encampment on the highway (usually various members of the Ayres family), drunk in charge of a horse and cart, drunk in charge of a traction engine, driving a traction engine at an improper speed ('I should say he was going at more than five miles an hour'), using obscene language (a crime mainly perpetrated by cattle drovers, but also by one Jonas Starr who, along with his brother, Job Starr, was no stranger to the Basingstoke Magistrates Court). On the night of 21 January 1883 PC Astridge saw Jonas standing in the doorway of the *Castle* public house, shouting, 'Come out you bloody fucking bitch. Who paid your fare to London?' –the cry of unrequited love that still echoes down the ages.

Examining the cards (Alan Turton)

Other cases concerned obtaining money by false pretences. An entertaining example of this offence was committed by John Spencer. On Wednesday 12 October 1881, PC Hurst saw John Spencer in the Market Square surrounded by a knot of people. His spiel was that he had a pack of plain white cards and each card had an invisible picture that would only become visible in a darkened room. He said that, because of the nature of the pictures, he was not allowed to sell them. But he had some torn up pieces of newspaper, and anyone who bought a piece of newspaper would be given a card. PC Hurst watched him sell five or six cards that way before deciding to pounce. PC Hurst arrested him and took him to the Police Station, where he was searched. The police found 1/10½d in copper, 2/6d in silver and 40 cards on him. That night, after dark, the policemen gathered round and examined the cards, probably in the hope of seeing some dirty pictures. The prisoner then admitted that the cards had nothing on them. The magistrates dismissed him with a caution.[11]

Despite this rich variety of misdemeanours, the cases that dominated the Petty Court in 1881, and gave the magistrates such a headache, were cases concerning the Salvation Army.

---

11   Minutes of the Basingstoke Petty Court, 1881–3.

WAR DECLARED

We may plausibly attribute the hostile attitude of secular Basingstoke to the displeasure we all feel when confronted by religious enthusiasm in which we do not happen to participate . . . people should not march around in places where they had reason to suppose that they would provoke a disturbance. To vex and annoy our neighbours is not, we are certain, the way to convert them.

Daily News, 29 March 1881

The Salvation Army came to Basingstoke in 1880. They announced their arrival by covering the town with big yellow posters, which read:

O Yes! O Yes! O Yes!
To all you sinners who it may concern;
Two Hallelujah Lasses,
Being a Detachment of the Salvation Army
Will open fire on Sin and Satan,
At the Factory, Brook Street, Basingstoke,
On Sunday, September 19th, 1880.[12]

The *Hants and Berks Gazette* welcomed the arrival of the Salvation Army. On 25 September 1880 it reported:

> Two Hallelujah Lasses, being a contingent of the Salvation Army, arrived in the town last week, and commenced a determined onslaught on Sunday morning. Services were held in the open air, and also in the old silk-mill in Brook-street, now termed the Salvation Factory. These have been continued during the week, and large crowds have been attracted to hear them. Whatever may be said of the Salvation Army, and however ridiculous their manner

---

12   Clements, Ken, *Two Feeble Women: The Early History of the Salvation Army in Basingstoke* (no publisher noted, *c.* 1995).

of proceeding may appear to some eyes, there can be no doubt that their efforts have in some places resulted in a large amount of good. Drunkards and swearers and people of the most vile and wretched character have through their influence been known to become sober and thoughtful men and women.

Page 2 of the *Gazette* for 30 October 1880 was largely taken up by an essay, 'Objections to the Salvation Army answered', referring to objections from the Church of England; and the *Gazette* for 20 November 1880 gave a full and glowing report of a Salvation Army meeting, headed 'The Salvation Army / Council of War in Basingstoke'.

In typical militaristic style, the *War Cry* for 2 October 1880 wrote of the 'Latest Advance' of the Army:

> On Sunday Captain [Clara] Green and her Lieutenant Happy Martha [Ellis] opened fire in Basingstoke. The results so far have been glorious victories. Captain Green reporting the account of the battle says 'The Almighty came down upon us and the people here did not know what to make of us' . . . The Salvation Factory proved too small to hold the people and Happy Martha held a meeting outside while the Captain fired away inside.

A report of one of the earliest meetings in the *War Cry* for 23 October 1880 quotes the 'glowing testimonies' of Basingstoke converts:

> 'Oh I am so happy, last year I was carried home drunk, cursing and swearing; today look at me' . . . One old lady, as she came to the front with clasped hands, looking the picture of Holy thankfulness said, 'You all know me! You know that we were the most drunken family in Basingstoke, but Oh, this dear army came, and they were the first that ever said Salvation to me. Now I am saved and my old man, bless him, who never used to come home sober is saved'.

It seems clear that the coming of the Salvation Army received an enthusiastic welcome from some quarters of the town. They were encouraged and supported by the town's Congregationalists, Baptists, Methodists and Quakers, as well as the *Hants and Berks Gazette*. The *War Cry* for 13 January 1881 reported that the Basingstoke Corps had sold 1,300 copies of the paper – quite impressive for a town with a population of only 6,681. The same edition of the *War Cry* boasted that, since the Army 'took up the position of attack' in Basingstoke, one publican had said, 'Since the Salvation Army came to 'stoke I do not sell quarts even, where I once sold barrels'. It commented, 'The enemy have held supreme sway here so long . . . [but]. . . God came down to deliver . . . The Basingstoke Soldiers have only to go on the lines of Holiness . . . and the whole of the town will be brought to Jesus' feet.'

THE ATTACKS BEGIN

Others were less enthusiastic. The Salvation Army had only been in the town for a week when, in the words of the *Hants and Berks Gazette:*

> Some people near the brewery in Brook-street thought the vocalists
> were thirsty on Monday evening [27 September], but instead
> of asking them to step in and try some of their double x, they
> discharged a mixture of stale beer and barm over the moving
> company, much to their mortification and disgust.[13]

The *Gazette* later said that the managers of the brewery knew nothing about the beer-throwing incident. Barm is the froth that forms on the top of fermenting malt liquors.

On 6 October 1880 there were further disturbances that resulted in Frank Powell, a bricklayer, appearing before the magistrates charged with being drunk and disorderly. Powell called a Salvation Army soldier named Thomas Martin as a witness. It was an unwise choice, as it transpired that Powell had struck Mr Martin and several others who were going round the streets in the Salvation Army procession. However Martin said he did not wish to press charges, as he believed that Powell was incited to act in a violent manner by the mob. In an ingenious plea for mitigation Powell said that he had joined the Salvation Army, and was sorry for his behaviour. This induced the Bench to take a lenient view of the case. He was fined 10s including costs.[14]

It is clear that harassing the Salvation Army had become the new Basingstoke pastime. In an opinion piece on 27 November, the *Hants and Berks Gazette* asked:

> When will the persecution to which the Salvation Army is subjected
> cease? . . . Had a pack of wolves been let loose on Wednesday
> evening [24 November] in the streets, their howling could not
> have been more fraught with much more annoyance than were the
> execrations, shouting and screaming of the rabble that surrounded
> the Salvationists in the Market-place, and subsequently favoured
> them with their company as they perambulated the different streets.
> I am informed that some miscreants tried to trip up the vocalists
> by means of a rope, besides resorting to other indignities . . . The
> Mayor and other occupants of the town are called upon to protect
> these people, and the respectable portion of the community are
> beginning to think that it is high time Superintendent Hibberd
> should have some instructions in this matter.

---

13   *Hants and Berks Gazette*, 2 October 1880.
14   Ibid, 16 October 1880.

There was further trouble the following Wednesday evening. Under the headline, 'EXTRAORDINARY BEHAVIOUR IN THE STREETS OF BASINGSTOKE', the *Hants and Berks Gazette* for 4 December 1880 described how 'an organised mob made a determined attack on [the Salvation Army] ranks near the Post Office [which was then in Wote Street]'. The mob was attempting to capture the Salvation Army's flag. It was said that £20 was offered for the capture of the flag.[15] In the darkness of the night, amid the chaos and confusion and buffeting and brawling, one of the lads managed to get hold of the pole, but the standard bearer kept a firm grip, while others managed to pull the lad away. Two of the gang grabbed hold of Captain Green and dragged her away, but she was quickly rescued by 'her trusty followers'. The *Gazette* reported that 'hats were knocked from heads and trampled beneath the feet of the surging crowd, and several of the Army were struck by stones.'

The Salvation Army held another procession the following evening. This resulted in the arrests of Gilbert Lawes, William Cottrell, John Cook, Joseph Bell, George Collins, George Carter, George Harris and William Doswell. The last four were Salvation Army soldiers. All eight appeared before the Magistrates, charged with causing an obstruction in London Street on the evening of 2 December. Police Superintendent Hibberd told the court that between seven and eight o'clock in the evening:

> There was a great crowd of people congregated at the top of London Street [according to Sergeant Waldren, there were about a thousand people there]. They quite blocked the place up. There was a great deal of noise and tumult. I gave them a caution and said it was utterly impossible for people to pass, and unless they desisted from blocking the highway, I should have to take proceedings against them . . . After that I particularly cautioned them in Wote Street . . . Collins and Carter were carrying a flag and they were going about six abreast. It was like a football match, one party was trying to go up London Street and the other group was trying to prevent them. Cottrell, Cook and Bell were disguised more or less. Cook had on the pair of false whiskers I produce, a tall hat and some flour on his face. Cook and Cottrell had some heavy sticks in their hands . . . There was a great deal of shouting. I had the day before asked Collins and Carter not to bring out the flag as it fluttered in horses' faces and as there was so much feeling against them.

Superintendent Hibberd said he thought both parties were as bad as each

---

15   Clements, Ken, *Two Feeble Women: The Early History of the Salvation Army in Basingstoke* (no publisher noted, *c.* 1995).

other. In view of the conflicting testimonies, all eight charges were dismissed.[16]

The following Sunday (5 December 1880) there was more trouble. The *War Cry* described the open air meeting held that afternoon outside the Town Hall where 'about 200 Salvation Soldiers were present and an assembly of nearly a thousand.' After the meeting the Army marched up and down London Street where 'the ruffians tried to take our colours but in vain . . . others acted as escort to the Salvation Soldiers in the march back to the barracks. Some of the Soldiers have been stoned, others bespattered with mud, red ochre and rubbish etc.' The following day they held another open air meeting where 'the street seemed filled with fierce Ephesian beasts who roared and mocked'. (This echoed the comments of John Wesley. When he visited Basingstoke in February 1759, he said the people reminded him of the wild beasts at Ephesus.) Captain Green and Happy Martha were unable to attend this meeting due to 'sickness caused by chemicals thrown into their faces by opponents.'[17]

That evening hundreds gathered in the Market Place expecting the Salvation Army to arrive. But the Army never came. So, in the words of George Woodman's diary, 'they made a rush for the Silk Mill and stormed the place.' George Woodman kept a diary from 1862 to 1932 from which he wrote an account of the riots in two documents he produced in 1928 and 1930, copies of which are in the Local Studies room in the Willis Museum. In the early 1880s he worked in Arkas Sapp's chemist's shop.

In Christmas Week, Captain Green and Happy Martha with a contingent of Salvationists from the Basingstoke Corps visited Overton to join the service at the Wesleyan Chapel there.

> Blue ochre, flour and dough were thrown at the singing procession.
> The noise of the opposition party became a nuisance, and their
> awful mockeries almost amounting to blasphemy were such as to
> be deplored. The Chapel, we hear, has since been closed to the
> Salvation Army.[18]

The next month the Great Blizzard of 1881 struck the south of England. On 17 and 18 January, fierce gales drifted the snow up to nine feet deep in places. All the roads from Basingstoke were blocked and trains were stuck in the snow. 120 men had to be employed to dig a passage through Sherborne Road. It is little surprising, therefore, that when the Salvation Army marched out on Saturday 22 January they were pelted with snowballs and chunks of ice.

It was the Salvation Army's policy to rotate their senior officers every

---

16   *Hants and Berks Gazette*, 11 December 1880.
17   *War Cry*, 18 December 1880.
18   *Hants and Berks Gazette*, 1 January 1881.

few months. So on 26 January 1881 Captain Green and Happy Martha left Basingstoke. Their replacements were two other lady officers, Captain Lizzie Rushforth and Lieutenant Cremond.

DISTURBANCES IN THE FACTORY

A letter in the *Gazette* of 29 January 1881 complained about the conduct of 'several young men' who visited the factory for the purpose of disrupting the service by 'using the most foul-mouthed language and a blasphemous expression.' This refers to another piece of Sunday afternoon entertainment the lads enjoyed. After harassing the Salvation Army's procession, they would follow the Army's supporters into the factory to disrupt the service. John Cook had been charged in December 1880 with 'having misbehaved himself in a place set apart for religious worship' by talking and laughing, and swearing when he was asked to leave.

John Wear or Wearn, described as 'a young man, residing at Worting Town End', was summonsed by Thomas Martin for using improper language at the factory during the hours of divine service on 30 January 1881. It appears that he was part of a group who wore paper streamers in their hats. They took it in turns to stand up in the middle of the service, to the laughter of their mates. Thomas Martin told the magistrates that 'he swore and behaved in an improper manner. I asked him to go out but he would not do so. He was cracking nuts, and when I asked him to leave off he said he only had one more. He said this several times when remonstrated with. He had white paper round his hat, and he interrupted the service continually. When he was finally told to leave, he said, "Mr Martin, you can go to buggery".'[19] Mayor Blatch sentenced him to prison for a week with hard labour, without the option of a fine, and told him that he was being treated leniently.

On 22 February 1881, George Harris, the Salvation Army's 'bouncer', brought a prosecution against John Jennings for causing a disturbance in the factory and using bad language when asked to leave. George Harris said that Jennings was misbehaving himself by talking and laughing. When asked to behave himself, he said loudly, 'You talk to my arse.' Harris said, 'He would not leave. I then forced him towards the door. There was a struggle there until a constable appeared.'[20]

The Mayor, William Henry Blatch, told Jennings that the Bench had come to the unanimous decision that, whenever a body of men were gathered together for religious worship, let it be in church or in chapel, they had a perfect right to be protected, and the Bench was determined to protect the Salvation Army in their own building. Jennings was fined £2

---

19   Minutes of the Basingstoke Petty Court, 1879–81.
20   Ibid.

with 11s 6d costs, or in default one month's hard labour. £2 11s 6d was an awful lot of money in those days. Jennings opted for the month.[21]

The Mayor's summing up in the Jennings case prompted Frederick Blunden, chemist and wine merchant of 6 Market Place to write to the Mayor as follows:

> After the decision of our local magistrates . . . where you stated that you are determined to protect . . . [the Salvation Army] . . . in their own building, I as a ratepayer claim the right of protection in my own building; for months past you have allowed them to annoy me by bawling in the Market Place three times on Sundays led by a woman of very doubtful character . . . and unless they are stopped, I shall appeal to the Home Secretary or take the law into my own hands. In either case you must put up with the consequences.[22]

On another occasion, the Salvation Army prosecuted John Clark for indecent behaviour during the celebration of divine service, and Clark issued a counter-summons accusing George Collins of assaulting him. After hearing an hour of claim and counterclaim that Collins used excessive force in evicting Clark, and that Clark disrupted the service by talking and laughing and singing the hymns in an excessively loud voice (to the amusement of his mates), Mayor Blatch, the Chief Magistrate, threw both cases out.

John Clark, a solicitor's clerk who worked for William Bayley, the town clerk, was aged 23 at the time. He appears to have been a mixture of a comedian and a barrack-room lawyer. He amused the courtroom by running rings round the prosecuting lawyer the Salvation Army had brought down from London. When the Salvation Army's lawyer called Daniel Goodall as a witness, Clark cross-examined him.

> *Clark*: You say you asked me to go out, and that I said, 'You can't make me go out'? Will you swear that I didn't say 'You can't legally put me out'?
>
> *Goodall*: I heard you say that he couldn't put you out.
>
> *Clark*: Do you mean to say I didn't use the word 'legally'?
>
> *Goodall*: You said 'Thee casn't put me out.' (*laughter*).
>
> *Clark* (*to the Magistrates' clerk*): I don't know whether you can spell that, sir. [Daniel Goodall came from Wootton St Lawrence.]

The *Gazette* reported that the court was packed, 'principally with people opposed to the movements of the Salvation Army', who greeted Collins and his companions with a storm of abuse as they left the court.

---

21   Minutes of the Basingstoke Petty Court, 1879–81 and *Hants and Berks Gazette*, 26 February 1881.

22   PRO HO 45/9607/A2886.

The Town Hall in c. 1881, with the Ship Inn in Church Street on the left.
(Hampshire County Council Museums & Arts Service)

In the Mayor's summing up, he said that if there has been a disturbance in the factory, or any other place of worship, 'we shall punish the delinquents most severely.'[23]

THE MASSAGAINIANS

When the Clark case was being heard at the Petty Sessions on Tuesday 1 March, one of the police overheard someone say that there would be a strong party on the streets that would put a stop to the Salvation Army's meeting in the Market Place the following evening. Superintendent Hibberd visited Captain Rushforth and advised her not to venture out that night. But she told him she was determined to go ahead.

On the Wednesday night, just as the Salvation Army were about to begin their service outside the Town Hall, a gang of about 100 rushed at them, completely routing most of the worshippers. Captain Rushforth and a small group of Salvationists were separated from the rest and 'were surrounded by the mob, who hustled them to and fro, making the most inhuman yells imaginable . . . the sounds were more similar to those which would be expected from a collection of wild beasts.' The gang tried to force Captain Rushforth into the *Ship* public house and, as a letter to the *Hants and Berks Gazette* of 5 March 1881 headed, 'Ruffianism in Basingstoke' surmised, 'I verily believe that there were scoundrels in the crowd panting

23 *Hants and Berks Gazette*, 5 March 1881.

for the blood of the young girl who leads the Salvation Army, and that nothing but the light of the lamps and the eyes of her friends prevented them from gratifying their fiendish appetites.' One can only speculate what would have happened to her had they got her inside the *Ship*.

However, she was rescued by some very brave Salvationists. They escaped down Church Street, followed by a crowd who 'filled the air with unearthly yells and shrieks. The language used was filthy in the extreme, and most repugnant to the feelings.' Once the crowd reached the factory, 'the shouting commenced with renewed vigour and we noticed more than one well-dressed individual joining in the unearthly chorus. Swearing and blasphemy – expressions the vilest that could possibly disgrace the human tongue – were made use of, enough to call down the very curse of God.'

The correspondent asked why the police made no attempt to rescue Captain Rushforth when she was nearly forced into the *Ship*, when they must have seen that her life was in danger. He asked whether it was 'possible that the ratepayers will allow a pack of depraved men and boys to commit gross outrages of this description without raising their voices in protest?'

Another correspondent wrote:

> Never was a time when the kingdom of Satan opposed himself with more violence and demoniacal hate to the kingdom of Christ than now.

The Salvation Army held a collection to take out a summons against John Clark for his involvement in that night's events, but decided against it as they concluded that, as they were not inside their place of worship, the worst punishment he could expect would be a fine.

The next evening, a crowd gathered in Brook Street, waiting for the Salvation Army to come out of their barracks. In a letter to the *Gazette*, 9 April, Richard Wallis said that when the Salvation Army attempted to leave,

> The poor fellows were pelted with clods, rubble dirt, etc, and after they managed to get inside, volleys of stones and brickbats were thrown at their door and inner partition to the endangering of some of their lives, accompanied by the foulest imprecations, their lamp was smashed, and this went on for over an hour.

One Salvationist was hit in the face by a stone.

Lizzie Rushforth wrote to the Home Secretary, enclosing cuttings from the *Hants and Berks Gazette*, requesting protection for the Salvation Army in Basingstoke. An internal Home Office note commented:

> It is the old story. The Salvation Army provokes a riot by processions and harangues in the streets and is much aggrieved

because the police cannot protect them from molestation. The
magistrates heard the cross-summonses and dismissed them both
giving good advice which neither party will take. There seems
nothing to enquire about.[24]

Richard Wallis also wrote to the Home Secretary. He wrote on 9
March, enclosing cuttings from the *Gazette*, including the 'Ruffianism in
Basingstoke' letter, as follows:

> As a last resort I take the liberty of addressing you on a subject which,
> if not dealt with properly now, may end in some people being maimed,
> or possibly loss of life . . . The liquor interest is strong in this Borough
> and some of those engaged in the traffic led the assault supported by
> the rowdy men and boys of this place . . . Now I take it there must
> be a law to meet this case: Stone's Justices Manual under 'Preaching'
> makes it clear to me what our duty is, but it comes to this – whether
> these people (some of Her Majesty's subjects) are to be protected
> from insult and injury. Any instructions addressed to me or to the
> Magistrates' Clerk, F. S. Chandler, would be very welcome.[25]

The Home Office forwarded Wallis's letter to the Mayor, asking for
comments. Mayor Blatch called a meeting of the magistrates, including
Richard Wallis. As a result, the existence of the letter became known all
round the town.

Mayor Blatch reported back to the Home Secretary that the magistrates
had discussed Richard Wallis's letter, and were unanimous that they were
taking the right course, 'Mr R Wallis alone in thinking differently.' He
continued:

> Since the advent of the Salvation Army here we have at times a
> difficult task to keep our Town quiet, but the magistrates have
> constantly done their very best to act with the strictest impartiality
> towards all . . . The letters in the local paper sent to you by Mr R
> Wallis were, I find, written to you by a young man, the reporter to the
> paper [This was almost certainly William Thompson.] . . . I believe
> the police have done their duty thoroughly with circumspection and
> firmness . . . No member of the Army has been locked up or fined
> even, and the decisions of the magistrates have met with almost
> universal approval of all moderate people in the town, on either side.
> I don't know what the 'Liquor interest' has specially to do with this
> matter, unless Mr R Wallis connects it with the letter [the Frederick
> Blunden letter] which I enclose received from a Wine and Spirit

24   TNA PRO HO 45/9607/A2886.
25   Ibid.

Mayor William Henry Blatch (Hampshire County Council
Museums & Arts Service)

Merchant in the Market Place who keeps a bar as well. Mr R Wallis is
a supporter of the Army and a teetotaller . . . I believe these people do
good in their place of worship, but when parading the streets in such
numbers, and more especially in the dark, that good is to a great extent
counterbalanced by the angry feelings called forth. We congratulated
ourselves on having done much better than other Towns, by adopting
moderate measures . . . I was sorry to find that Mr Wallis has opened
up this question in the way he has . . . We have severely punished
parties who have rendered themselves liable by annoying those folks
in their place of worship . . . nor have we refused them protection
to the utmost of our ability; but I have also persuaded them to act
less aggressively and with greater circumspection. I have had many
complaints of the annoyance to invalids, children, and persons who
value quiet in their homes, caused by the Army singing so loudly

through the streets . . . I may say that our opinions are not swayed by
political or party religious feelings which you will better understand
when I tell you that of the six magistrates, the two Mr Wallises I
consider Radicals, I have been a moderate Liberal all my life and the
Ex Mayor and two others are Conservatives. Three of us are Non
Conformists and three Churchmen.[26]

On Sunday 13 March the Salvation Army announced that there would
be a procession the following evening. They asked their supporters to meet
them at the bottom of Chapel Street. They would then march up Wote
Street to the Market Place and return to their barracks along Winchester
Street, down New Street, through Cross Street, Church Street and Brook
Street.
On the Monday evening, according to the *Gazette*, they were:

> . . . once again set upon in a brutal and inhuman manner by their
> enemies . . . along the whole route, the conduct of certain well-
> known ruffians [including Ernest Fitzgerald, Frank Powell and
> Frank Chalk][27] led on by people occupying a higher position in the
> social scale, but with morals equally as corrupt was blackguardedly
> in the extreme. The members of the Army attempted to sing, but
> their voices were drowned by the horrible yells and groans of the
> rabble. At the top of New-street the enemy made a charge on the
> ranks of the Army and succeeded in breaking the company into two
> parts. The captain at the same time being divided from her frail
> lieutenant. Considerable confusion ensued after this, and members
> of the Army were handled in a rough manner. Mr Bridgeman, a
> prominent supporter of the lady officers, took charge of Lieutenant
> Cremond, who is of slight build and apparently very delicate, but
> his kind protection was insufficient to prevent a scoundrel striking
> her a blow in the back, from the effects of which she suffered
> considerably. Mr Greenaway and a young man named Harris were
> also knocked about, and the presence of the police had little or no
> effect in keeping the mob in order. [Ernest Fitzgerald thumped
> George Harris in Church Street, but alleged that Harris had hit
> him first.] It is only fair to the Superintendent, however, to say that
> he went to the commander and asked her to place herself under his
> protection, which she refused to do, preferring to remain with her
> soldiers, even though the odds were against them.[28]

---

26   Ibid.
27   *Hants and Berks Gazette*, 26 March 1881.
28   *Hants and Berks Gazette*, 19 March 1881.

On Thursday 17 March a small handbill was posted on pub windows and other places around town. It read as follows:

War Declared.
Massagainians to the Rescue.
Meet in the Market-square on Sunday morning at ten o'clock,
to oppose Dirty Dick's Army.
Colours – Union Jack
Watchword – Disperse.
Headquarters, Basingstoke, March 1881.

Dirty Dick is thought to be a reference to Richard Wallis.

It has been suggested that the handbill urged the townsfolk to 'Mass Again against the Salvation Army', and that was the origin of the term, 'Massagainian'. But it is likely that they were calling themselves Massagainians before the handbill was printed.

It appears that this handbill may have given rise to a handbill from the opposite camp. At a meeting of the Watch Committee on 7 April, Councillor Dunn criticised the magistrates for not taking action to identify and prosecute the author of the handbill. (There were strong hints that the author was one of the Adams brothers from the Victoria Brewery.) Mayor Blatch asked Councillor Dunn which bill he was referring to, pointing out that two bills had been issued: one from the Massagainians; and another calling on 500 young men to come forward and defend the Salvation Army.[29]

---

29   *Hants and Berks Gazette*, 9 April 1881.

THE BATTLE OF CHURCH SQUARE

IS THE POWER OF THE BASINGSTOKE
MAGISTRATES PARALYSED?

Never within the memory of the oldest resident has the town of Basingstoke presented such a spectacle as it did on Sunday. The usual quiet of the day gave place to a reign of anarchy and disorder. The aspect of the Market-place, of New-street and Church-street, before the hour of morning service would have been highly discreditable to the town a hundred years ago. And what took place in the afternoon, just about three o'clock, in the Church-square, under the shadow of the ancient pile of St Michael's, and in the presence of the graves of our ancestors, must be characterised as a most disgraceful proceeding, the parallel of which could scarcely be furnished by any town in England.

Leading article in the Hants and Berks Gazette, *26 March 1881.*

March 20th 1881 Sunday. Between nine and ten a.m. some 200 or so of the roughest characters in the town assembled in the Market Place for the purpose of molesting the Salvation Army. Most of them had sticks under their arms and short pipes in their mouths. The numbers greatly increased until it had reached about 1,000. At the same time a great number of respectable people went out and headed the SA and protected them on either side . . . By this time the number had increased to about 2,000. Some tried to keep their footings while others tried to push them down. Some windows were broken on Church Street. In the afternoon about 1.40 p.m. the mob assembled again. They were a drunken rabble. They turned the SA into Church Square and broke their ranks. They knocked their heads about with sticks, kicked them and many of them being drunk would have made short work of the SA had it not been for the timely aid of sympathisers. I saw a man being led away with his arm broken and head cut, another with his neck bleeding and another with his head cut open. There were bleeding heads and faces in all directions. On this occasion, the police and the Mayor W. H. Blatch, himself a brewer, stood by and did nothing. Among the leaders of the mob were the Adams Brothers from the Victoria Brewery. John Soper, Arkas Sapp, the Rev. Barron, Richard Wallis and S. Wallis and other members of the Wallis family were attacked as they walked with the SA.

George Woodman's diary, Willis Museum.

The day of 20 March 1881 opened to a clear bright Sunday morning. The town was peaceful and quiet. Sometime after nine o'clock knots of men and boys began to converge on the Market Place in answer to the Massagainians' summons. By ten o'clock 'an immense crowd' had gathered, waiting for the Salvation Army to arrive.

At ten o'clock the Salvation Army left the factory. They marched along Brook Street and up Church Street, singing hymns. They were half way along Church Street when a cry broke out from the Market Place, 'Here they come!' The Massagainians charged down the hill towards the Salvation Army. Spotting the enemy running towards them, the Salvation Army wheeled round into Cross Street. The Massagainian horde juddered to a halt and turned back up Church Street. They raced along Winchester Street to intercept the Salvation Army in New Street.

With the Massagainians moving down New Street, led by Harry Barkham carrying the Union Jack, and the Salvation Army headed by their protectors moving up the street, a collision was inevitable. Just before the two sides clashed, Henry Barron, Councillor George Dunn, Mark Trevethick, Minister of the Primitive Methodist Chapel in Flaxfield Road, and some others detached themselves from the Salvation Army procession and rushed into the gap. By frantic gestures and anguished cries above the roar of the crowd, they urged the Army to keep as near to the left hand side of the road as possible to make room for the Massagainians to pass.

The Massagainians had no intention of crossing to the other side of the road, and the clash took place outside the Mechanics' Institute. Both sides pushed against each other. In the confusion Charles Elms, described in Court later as a 'muscular Salvationist', managed to wrest the Massagainians' flag away from Barkham, and in the struggle the staff was broken. The Massagainians made a fierce rush at the Salvationists and, after a tussle in which blows were freely exchanged and the Salvation Army's flagstaff was broken in three, the Massagainians managed to recapture their flag. To make Elms let go of the Massagainians' flag, Harry Barkham hit him with such force that he broke Elms's arm.

Eventually the Salvationists managed to force their way up New Street, surrounded by, what the *Gazette* described as 'hired roughs' who pushed and hustled them, 'yelling and hooting in a most disgraceful manner'. From the corner of New Street and Winchester Street the Salvation Army and their supporters tried to push their way through the crowd to the Market Place, where they had planned to hold their service. But the crowd continued to push and jostle them. During the course of the short distance along Winchester Street the Massagainians kept breaking the Army's ranks. The leaders had to keep stopping while their followers fought their way through the obstructing crowd before they could move forward again. Every upstairs window in Winchester Street was filled with spectators, some horrified by the desecration of the Victorian Sabbath taking place in their own street, while others were no doubt enjoying the free entertainment.

When the Salvation Army eventually reached the top of Church Street, the Massagainians blocked their path to the Market Place and pushed them down the steep slope of Church Street. Many of the Army's supporters tried to protect the Army by setting their backs against the surging crowd to try to check the onward rush. In the stampede one unfortunate was pushed through the plate-glass window of the Little Dustpan furniture shop, another was knocked down and trampled upon, and 'many detached struggles and conflicts occurred' all the way down Church Street.

Once they reached the bottom of Church Street by St Michael's, the Massagainians were content to escort the Salvation Army to their factory, having succeeded in their objective of preventing that morning's Market Place service. Once the Salvation Army reached the safety of their factory, the Massagainians dispersed to their various pubs to refresh themselves for Round Two in the afternoon.

From about half-past one that afternoon, groups of Massagainians and the idly curious began to leave their pubs and strolled to the Market Place, where they had agreed to regroup. By two o'clock the Market Place was heaving with Massagainians and their hangers on. As many of them had been drinking for several hours, they were in a boisterous and excitable mood. While they were waiting for the next piece of action, they amused themselves by singing a parody of the Salvation Army hymn, 'Will You Go?'

As soon as their scouts reported that the Salvation Army had left their factory and were marching along Church Street, the Massagainians, led by Edward, Charles and Valentine Adams of the Victoria Brewery, crowded down Church Street towards the Army with their repaired Union Jack to the fore.

The Salvation Army procession, 150 strong, led by Major Moore and Captain Jordan, was reinforced by the leaders of the Nonconformist chapels and other sympathisers who had rallied to support the Army. When Major Moore saw the huge crowd of Massagainians heading towards them, he wheeled his soldiers into Church Square, where they formed a defensive circle and started to sing a hymn.

The Massgainians gave what the *Gazette* described as 'a most unearthly yell' and charged into the Square. Thus began what became known as the Battle of Church Square, or, as the *Saturday Review* described it, 'The Basingstoke Brawl'. [30]

The Massagainians tore through the Salvation Army's defenders. Their overpowering weight of numbers was too much for the Salvation Army soldiers who were trying to maintain their circle. The Massagainians soon broke the circle and the scene became one of a confused mass of red-faced people pushing and shoving against one another. It wasn't long before blows

---

30 *Saturday Review*, 2 April 1881.

The Battle of Church Square
(Alan Turton)

were exchanged, which quickly developed into a free fight. The police and other witnesses estimated that there were about 3,000 people crowded into the Square, many of whom were involved in the fighting.

On the Massagainian side, the Adams brothers were in the thick of the fighting; as were the brothers Frank, John and Herbert Wallis and their cousin, Sterry Wallis, who were supporting the Salvation Army. In the words of Charles Doman, 'The Wallises were very busy with their fists.' The *Gazette*, somewhat admiringly, described how Frank Wallis dealt one of the Massagainians 'three or four blows straight from the shoulder'.

John Wallis claimed that Valentine Adams ran up to him and hit him with his fist. Valentine Adams said that he was the victim of an unprovoked attack by John and Herbert Wallis. What seems to be indisputable is that John Wallis threw Adams to the ground:

. . . and getting a firm hold on his throat attempted to throttle him. This led the gentleman's relations and friends to come to the rescue, and then the melée became pretty general, and high, low, rich or poor had to defend themselves in the best way they could, the Mayor himself receiving some ugly knocks.

During the attempts to rescue Valentine Adams, Edward Adams hit Frank Wallis. As John Fennell stormed in to assist the Wallises, who were by now outnumbered, Edward Adams punched him three times with his fist, shouting, 'Down with the Wallises'. Fennell, who was a much bigger man, grabbed hold of Adams, tearing his shirt open, and dragged him towards PC Mears. Charles Doman attempted to rescue Adams, but before he could reach Fennell, John Wallis thumped him in the eye. When Fennell tried to deliver Adams to PC Mears, PC Mears told him to go away. On which, Adams, by now bleeding from the neck, shouted, 'Back up Basingstoke!' Charles Adams punched Fennell in the face, causing blood to flow from his mouth. Fennell later said, 'I think about a dozen commenced thrashing me with sticks and cudgels, and they didn't forget to kick me. I was bruised from head to foot.'

In the meantime, other battles were raging. Elms, the unfortunate Salvationist who had his arm broken in New Street that morning, had his head cut open in the afternoon when Daniel Hatton hit him with a stick. Edward Clayton was knocked down by someone's fist and trampled on and kicked. His clothes were torn and he was covered in blood. Someone helped him up, but shortly afterwards Ernest Fitzgerald punched him in the eye. Clayton was also hit over the head by Harry Barkham with his flagstaff. Thomas Emery hit George Collins, cutting his lip and breaking one of his teeth. Someone gave Henry Yeates, the Primitive Methodist Minister's son, a black eye. William Hudson, a music teacher, said that around 30 or 40 of the Massagainians were wielding sticks. He said they attacked the members of the Army indiscriminately, and Charles Adams had struck him in the face. Hudson also accused Councillor George Tubb, the landlord of the *Black Boy*, of assaulting him. The *Hampshire Chronicle* reported that 'sticks were freely used, and blood flowed from many a head and nose, and hats, particularly high ones, were demolished in a most reckless manner.' Edward Clayton said he saw several people 'with blood on their faces, and others with their teeth knocked out.'

Eventually Mayor Blatch and Superintendent Hibberd managed to persuade the leaders of the Salvation Army to return to their factory. As the Salvation Army quit the field, the Massagainians gave three cheers for the Mayor and marched off in triumph, singing their parody of the Salvation Army hymn.

That evening the Massagainians gathered in the Market Place in the

Arthur Hailstone c. 1881 (Hampshire County Council Museums & Arts Service)

expectation that the Salvation Army would hold its open-air service at seven o'clock. But the Salvationists had the good sense to remain in their factory. So the Massagainians dispersed to their various pubs.[31]

According to Arthur Hailstone, reminiscing in 1945, that same evening at the service in the London Street Congregational Church, as Henry Barron stood up in the pulpit, he announced, 'Brethren, I feel more like fighting, than preaching tonight.' Arthur has good reason to remember that night. As he was walking home after the service, John Clark recognised him as one of the Salvation Army's defenders that afternoon, and laid him out with a blow between the eyes. The following day, in Arthur's words, he had 'two lovely black eyes.'[32]

---

31 *Hampshire Chronicle*, 26 March 1881; *Hants and Berks Gazette*, 26 March 1881, 9 April 1881, 16 April 1881, 7 May 1881, and 14 May 1881; *Report of the Proceedings before the Magistrates, on May 3rd and 9th, 1881* (no publisher noted).
32 Manuscript paper, *The Salvation Army Riots*, written by Arthur Hailstone, then in his 86th year, on 1 May 1945 for the London Street Congregational Church.

'THE EVIL INFLUENCE OF BASINGSTOKE'

News of the riot was picked up by the news agencies and fed to the national and provincial press. The *Western Mail* (Cardiff) for 22 March 1881 ran with the following story:

> A serious disturbance took place on Sunday morning at Basingstoke. As the members of the Salvation Army were parading the streets, a number of roughs, led on by several young men of good social position, charged the ranks of the Army again and again. The Mayor and the whole of the police force could not control the mob. In the afternoon the proceedings were even more riotous. A number of persons had their heads broken and their limbs fractured.

Other papers, including the *Preston Guardian*, *Reynolds' Newspaper*, and the *Birmingham Daily Post* ran stories on similar lines. Basingstoke was getting famous.

On 23 March, General Booth sent a memorandum to the Home Secretary:

> . . . about a month ago, the Publicans commenced to incite the roughs of the town to meet together and interrupt, and then attack our people, offering a reward of some pounds to any who would steal our flag.
>
> Thus encouraged, the mob rapidly increased in number and violence, and a fortnight ago a dreadful scene occurred in the Market Place. Several of our people were hurt, and the Police, by their presence and inaction, and otherwise, encouraged the mob.
>
> The Mayor (— Blanche [*sic*], Esq.), a member of the firm of May & Co., brewers, was appealed to to issue instructions to the Police to prevent a recurrence of these disorders, but did not do so; and, accordingly, the Publicans issued bills and took further steps to organise the roughs.
>
> On Sunday last (March 20), the Publicans having displayed copies of the following bill . . . [the text of the Massagainian handbill of 17 March] . . . in their windows, 'treated' all comers, and, as our people were walking in procession towards the Market Place, the mob, led by Messrs V., C. W., & E. Adams (also brewers) attacked with sticks, &c., our people. One man had his arm broken, another his jaw broken, and one had his head broken open. Many were brutally kicked and seriously injured, and, but for the interposition of several gentlemen who are in sympathy with us, things would have been worse still.
>
> The Mayor was present during the whole of this scene. He made

John Bird, founder and editor of the Hants and Berks Gazette, *drawn by his grandson, Wilfred J. Bird. (Basingstoke Gazette)*

no attempt to interpose, nor did the Police who were with him; and, although it had been known for several days that this attack was intended, no precautions had been taken. The Mayor was three times cheered by the mob, as he stood a spectator of the riot.

There undoubtedly has been, and is, a conspiracy, to which the Mayor is seemingly a party, to encourage the mob in the creation of a state of things which can then be used as an excuse for attempting by law to stop our work in the streets.

To nearly all the above facts the Senior Magistrate of the town, Richard Wallis, Esq, J.P., will bear witness.[33]

On the evening of 21 March, something called the Working Men's Indignation Meeting was held in the teetotal British Workman club room to protest against the persecution of the Salvation Army. It was attended by John Bird, Thomas Burberry, Councillors Kingdon, Sapp and Schofield, Rev Henry Barron, Rev Henry Yeates and other leading nonconformists.It is not clear how many actual British workmen were there.

---

33   TNA PRO HO 45/9607/A2886.

John Bird told the meeting that he was heartily in sympathy with the work of the Salvation Army and wished it God Speed. This would have been no surprise to anyone who had been reading the *Gazette* for the past few months. He blamed the Mayor and the Magistrates for inaction. Mr Bridgeman, who so gallantly protected Lieutenant Cremond on 14 March, said he 'loved the Salvation Army because they were pledged before high heaven to sweep strong drink from the face of the earth'.

That same evening, a small detachment of the Salvation Army left Basingstoke 'to storm Odiham and make a stronghold of the town' by holding a meeting in the 'preaching room of the Baptist cause'. During the service, a gang made up of 'married men with children, and young men and lads who have lately left school' insulted the worshippers with 'foul and abusive language', broke the windows and threw rotten eggs. An Odiham resident writing to the *Hants and Berks Gazette* considered that the gang was 'doubtless impelled by the evil influence of Basingstoke.'[34]

The *Gazette* on 26 March was full of the stories of the riot. In its opinion columns it noted:

> The chief topic of conversation in the town this week has been the vicious attack on Sunday last of the Massagainians under Captains Adams and others on the unarmed Salvation Army. Everyone has been asking why the police did not interfere . . . Is it true that the Mayor who was also present and saw blows struck took no one in charge? The ringleaders of the mobocrasy, who are responsible for Sunday's outrage, are well known. If the authorities had thought proper to have done so, they could have punished those parties who issued the bill inciting the riot. And if the police had done their duty, they would have seized those who were using cudgels so mercilessly on Sunday afternoon.

It added that, although the police were present 'in strong force, they might as well have been at home with their wives, for any effect that their presence had with the roughs', and that, 'we could not shut our eyes to the fact that the roughs of Basingstoke were not altogether impervious to the bribes thrown out by some licensed victuallers in the town.'

Major Moore wrote to the *Gazette*:

> There can be no two opinions as to the mob being gathered, sustained and led on by men interested in the drink traffic; and the marvel to us is that any man claiming one spark of human feeling can, after such an exhibition as that of Sunday, ever touch the cursed thing again.[35]

---

34 *Hants and Berks Gazette*, 26 March 1881.
35 Ibid.

An unnamed correspondent wrote:

> Yesterday I could scarcely believe myself in dear old England. The good old Cromwell might well blush could he have witnessed such a scene on the very spot where he fought so bravely for our liberty. Are we prepared to let it slip from our feeble fingers and leave to our sons only a heritage of shame? Liberties won for us years ago, to be parted with because money and beer have bought the consciences of a few hundreds of our poor fallen fellow creatures. These are to be pitied more than blamed. Others who have used them as their tools will have to answer for the sins of these deluded ones, as well as their own. That horrid traffic, 'England's curse', is at the bottom of it . . . Satan is rousing the indignation of his earthly agents.[36]

36 Ibid.

READING THE RIOT ACT

When the rulers met and conspired together as to how they could destroy Jesus
the tableau that illustrated it to me was . . . a scene which I witnessed not many
years ago in Basingstoke . . . The Mayor read the Riot Act, and in a few minutes
a troop of artillerymen, mounted and armed, were trampling their way through
the crowd, which fled in all directions. But there is no end to the tableaux that
might be prepared from the record of the struggle of the Salvation Army against
the publicans and their backers on the Bench. Christ before Herod received quite
as kindly a treatment as that which many a Salvationist captain received from the
hands of an English magistrate.

W. T. Stead, The Story that Transformed the World
or the Passion Play at Oberammergau, *1890*

Apart from one incident, all was quiet in Basingstoke the following week.
The Salvation Army, reckoning that discretion was the better part of valour,
held their mid-week services in the factory, instead of in the streets. The
only breach of the peace happened on the Tuesday night when Ann Rogers
of Windover Street and her son and daughter, William and Sarah, were
arrested for being drunk and disorderly. In connection with a temperance
conference being hosted in Basingstoke that week, a teetotal band from
Southampton was playing music in the Market Place. Or they were until
the Rogers family turned up and started swearing at them. When William
began 'brandishing a stick in a threatening manner', the band picked up
their instruments and ran, taking refuge in the Corn Exchange.[37]

When the Salvation Army announced that it would be parading through
the town as usual the following Sunday, the town was abuzz with speculation,
expecting a repeat of the previous Sunday's violence. The excitement was
increased when it was discovered that a detachment of the Royal Horse
Artillery, on the march from Christchurch to London, would be billeted
in the town on the Sunday. They entered the town on the Saturday around
noon. Mayor Blatch asked Major Curson, the Commanding Officer, to
stand his men in readiness as 'he had reliable information that there was
likely to be rioting between the Salvation Army and the roughs of the
place' the following day.[38] The Mayor also took the precaution of swearing

---

37 *Hants and Berks Gazette,* 2 April 1881.
38 Report from Major Curson to the Secretary of State for War. TNA PRO HO
45/9607/A2886.

in 100 of 'the principal tradesmen of the town' as special constables. Also on the Saturday the delightfully named Colonel Pepper and Major Moore arrived in town to take command of the Salvation Army.

On the morning of Sunday 27 March 1881 the residents of Church Street were treated to the sight of the special constables marching down the hill from the Town Hall to meet the Salvation Army at the corner of Brook Street. According to the *Hampshire Chronicle*:

> They were given a stick much resembling a plain deal rolling pin, not worth more than threepence, and a piece of white tape, with the words 'Special Constable' in black, to put round their arms. Some, it seemed, placed these upside down, provoking taunts that these officers of the peace could not read, and that their garters were not tied in the right place.[39]

The Salvation Army and their sympathisers, headed by Nonconformist Ministers and with Colonel Pepper, Major Moore and Captain Jordan in command of their soldiers, set off from the factory at ten o'clock, singing 'There is a Fountain Filled with Blood'. They marched up Church Street, through the Market Place, down Wote Street, and back along Brook Street to their factory, four abreast, singing hymns, with the Special Constables marching with them sullen and embarrassed, protecting the Army's front, their rear and either side. Behind them marched the Massagainians, playing a variety of instruments, including tin whistles, trumpets, 'one or two brass instruments that appeared to have been dug out of the earth', fog horns, saucepan lids, a clarinet and tin cans full of stones. Those without instruments helped to drown the hymn singing by hooting, yelling and laughing, and singing obscene songs. It must have been a hilarious sight.

Apart from the noise, the procession passed off peacefully. The Massagainians had made their point that, if the Salvation Army can be given the right to disturb the peace of the Basingstoke Sunday morning by marching round the town singing hymns, then they had a similar right to make their rough music. If they created enough nuisance, processions might get banned.

Once the Salvation Army was safely back at the factory, the crowd dispersed: the Nonconformists to their chapels; and the Massagainians to their pubs to discuss the arrangements for the afternoon.

As Henry Barron was walking down Church Street to his home in Essex Road, after leading the morning service at the London Street Congregational Church, George Tubb came storming out of the *Black Boy*, shouting at him, 'We will give you a bloody hiding this afternoon,' at the same time giving emphasis to his threat by way of gesticulation.[40]

---

39   *Hampshire Chronicle*, 2 April 1881.
40   *Hants and Berks Gazette*, 2 April 1881.

'Scranny Hockey' wielding his stick and brown paper – and his beer. (Alan Turton)

In the meantime, around three-quarters of the special constables called on the Mayor and told him they would not continue to protect 'such a set of damned hypocrites'. Some even joined forces with the Massagainians that afternoon. As the *Hampshire Chronicle* explained:

> . . . [the special constables,] . . . many of them staunch Churchmen, brought from their homes and prevented from attending their morning devotions, in order to protect the public peace, found themselves forming an escort for a religious sect they neither belonged to nor approved of, and which had in their ranks only a small number of ratepayers of the town; and to many the position was humiliating in the extreme. The further they went, the greater the grievance seemed to become; and by the time the Salvationists were safely lodged in their place of worship, and the preservers of the peace were marching back to the Market-place, murmurs of discontent could be heard on either side.[41]

Just before two o'clock the Salvation Army assembled outside their factory, four deep and ready to march again. At the same time some 3,000 Massagainians and their supporters were pouring down Church Street and into Brook Street, headed by the Massagainian band. They were led by an old man, 'bent with age or rheumatism', who was known as 'Scranny Hockey'. The Massagainians had plied him with drink and adopted him as their mascot. He led the way, 'bearing aloft on a stick a large piece of broken brown paper'.

---

41   *Hampshire Chronicle*, 2 April 1881.

In the words of the *Hants and Berks Gazette*:

> The roughs filled nearly the whole of Church-street. It is
> estimated that there were between two and three thousand of
> them, their ranks having been augmented by large numbers from
> the surrounding villages since the morning procession. That
> they had been well supplied with beer there can be no doubt:
> indeed, it is impossible that many of them would have taken the
> trouble to traverse several miles to get into the town, had not some
> temptation been held out to them. With regard to the characters
> of these men, it is scarcely necessary to say anything. To say that
> they were of the public-house class will be of sufficient indication
> to our readers of the sort of men that composed the mob. Those
> of the leaders who busied themselves in enlisting such a vast
> collection of men know very well that it would be of little use to
> go anywhere but to the public-house to obtain recruits for such
> a cause. As to the special constables, it was evident that some
> alteration had taken place to their mode of action. Instead of
> marching down in order as in the morning, they were only to be
> seen here and there among the body of the roughs.[42]

The Salvation Army procession had only got as far as May's Brewery
when they saw the Massagainians coming towards them. The Salvation
Army turned round towards their barracks and stood two deep against the
wall, waiting for the Massaganians to pass. Instead of heading straight on,
the Massagainian band turned round as soon as they passed the last of the
line of Salvationists. They then marched backwards and forwards in front
of the Army, playing their instruments and shouting insults, preventing the
Salvationists from moving either way.

This carried on for some time until one of the Massagainians pushed
another into Captain Jordan. When he collided with the Captain, he
grabbed hold of him for support, and appeared to be pulling the captain
away from the Army and into the crowd. On that, one of the special
constables cried out, 'Violence!', and others took up the call, 'Blows struck',
loud enough for the Mayor to hear. The Mayor then read the Riot Act:

> Our Sovereign Lady the Queen chargeth and commandeth all
> persons, being assembled, immediately to disperse themselves, and
> peaceably to depart to their habitations, or to their lawful business,
> upon the pains contained in the Act made in the first year of King
> George, for preventing tumults and riotous assemblies. God Save the
> Queen!

---

42   *Hants and Berks Gazette*, 2 April 1881.

As soon as the Mayor read the Riot Act, Edward Adams was heard to shout, 'That's all we want.' The Massagainians started cheering and made way for the Salvation Army to file back into the factory. The Massagainians then marched off, singing 'Rule Britannia'.

The *Gazette* hinted that this result was planned. It said the Salvation Army were 'the victims of a crafty plot. No violence was used, no blows were struck, and there was not the slightest pretence for reading the Riot Act.'

After he read the Riot Act, Mayor Blatch scribbled a note to Major Curson:

> The Riot Act having been read, I request you will as soon as possible send a sufficient force of the men under your command to quell the Riot, and to assist the Authorities in clearing the streets and restoring order to the Town.[43]

The Mayor handed the note to PC Simpson, who ran all the way up Church Street to the Market Place, where the artillerymen were mustered in readiness for this eventuality.[44] On receiving the note from PC Simpson, 20 mounted horsemen and 40 foot soldiers charged down Church Street in readiness to do battle.

Instead of the hostile mob they were expecting, they met a noisy, boisterous and good natured crowd of Massagainians, rejoicing in their victory. Although it took about an hour to clear the streets, there was no real trouble. Only one person was arrested. James Morris of Mapledurwell had walked to Basingstoke either out of curiosity or in the expectation of free beer. He had obviously partaken too copiously of the latter. He was charged with being drunk and riotous in London Street and had to be carried, kicking and struggling, to New Street Police Station. Found guilty of disorderly behaviour after the Riot Act had been read and hindering the authorities in trying to keep the peace, he was fined £1, or 14 days' hard labour in default. He was given a fortnight to pay.

The following evening at about 8.30, many people living near the centre of the town heard two loud bangs. These were caused by someone smashing the plate glass window and the pane in the door of the *Gazette* office in Church Street. Fragments of glass flew across the publishing office. As she stood behind the counter, a piece of glass struck Mrs Bird in the hand, 'causing it to bleed copiously'. It was said that this was the result of a reward for two barrels of beer for the first person to break the *Gazette*'s windows.

---

43   Report from Major Curson to the Secretary of State for War. TNA PRO HO 45/9607/A2886.

44   I owe the information about PC Simpson's role from Tom Wilson, PC Simpson's great-great grandson, who supplied me with a copy of PC Simpson's obituary cut from a 1937 newspaper (probably *Hants and Berks Gazette*).

The same evening, as Captain Jordan was walking to the railway station, a gang of about 30 people, including Albert Lansley, Frank Powell, William Phillips, Richard Humphries and led by Ernest Fitzgerald, followed him down Wote Street, using 'threatening and abusive language'. They were closely followed by Sergeant Waldren and PC Hurst. When they got to the bridge over the River Loddon, Fitzgerald stood in front of the Captain, blocking his way. (Captain Jordan told the magistrates that Fitzgerald 'got in front of me and obstructed my passage'.) Fitzgerald turned to his mates and said, 'Let's throw the bugger into the river', which was a steep drop of some five feet below the level of Wote Street. Sergeant Waldren rushed over and told Fitzgerald to leave Jordan alone. Fitzgerald repeated, 'Let's throw the bugger into the river. There's only two bloody policemen, and there's enough of us to manage them.' Fortunately for all concerned, Fitzgerald's companions did not adopt his suggestion. The two policemen escorted the Captain to the station.

When the case came to court on 5 April, Fitzgerald's lawyer asked for Richard and Arthur Wallis to be removed from the Bench as they were active supporters of the Salvation Army. Mayor Blatch refused the request. Because Fitzgerald did not actually hit Captain Jordan, the initial charge of assault and battery was thrown out. But Fitzgerald, Lansley, Powell and Phillips were found guilty of using threatening and abusive language and were each fined 30 shillings plus four shillings costs with 14 days' hard labour in default.

Richard Humphries' evidence for the defence is worth quoting in part:

> I remember Monday, March the 28th. I was one of the riotous mob. I saw [Fitzgerald] go up to the railway station and he went up the steps; the Sergeant gave him a shove and put him back . . . I saw the Sergeant partly draw his stave, and Fitzgerald his fog-horn.

During the court proceedings, Edward Clayton stepped forward to say something to the Salvation Army's solicitor. Fitzgerald turned to Clayton and in the full hearing of the courtroom told him he would 'smash his bloody head'.[45]

Ernest Fitzgerald appears to have been quite a character. Apart from his Massagainian activities, he was no stranger to the Basingstoke Magistrates Court. In August 1880 he was summonsed for committing an assault in the *Harrow* public house. In January 1881 he was charged with fighting in the *Ship* and refusing to leave the premises. He appeared before the court on several occasions for being at the centre of trouble in various pubs and for fighting in the street, including fighting in the Lesser Market on 31 August 1881 and being drunk and disorderly and breaking the windows of the *Rose and Crown* on 26 November 1881.

---

45   *Hants and Berks Gazette*, 9 April, 1881.

In July 1881 Frances Jones of Windover Street applied to the magistrates, complaining that Ernest was the father of her illegitimate daughter born on 22 February 1881, and that he had stopped paying the two shillings a week he had agreed to pay towards the child's upkeep. When both parties appeared before the magistrates on 1 November 1881, Frances Jones complained that Ernest had only given her eight shillings since the baby was born. Ernest said he was paying her two shillings a week, but she had abused him so frequently of late that he wouldn't give her any more money. Frances said that every time she asked Fitzgerald for money, he was in the habit of giving her two black eyes. In the full hearing of the court Ernest said, 'I'll give you another if you don't look out.' The magistrates ordered him to pay two shillings a week until the child was thirteen. To which Ernest replied, 'And the next time she abuses me, you'll grant a summons, won't you?' Frances responded, 'And the next time he gives me two black eyes, I shall want a summons against he.'[46]

The only other reference I can find for Frances Jones is in a report of a disturbance in the *Royal Exchange* on 28 May 1881 involving Ernest Fitzgerald, Henry Rawlings and William Phillips. It started when Ernest entered the pub 'with a woman named Jones' just before closing time. When George Brown, the landlord, refused to serve them, 'they both made use of bad language' and refused to leave the pub. PC Simpson was called in to evict them, but they started pushing the constable round the bar. One witness said that, 'The bother was all in consequence of a woman.'[47]

To add to his repertoire of misdemeanours, in November 1882 Ernest was convicted of poaching. There are undoubtedly other offences that I am not aware of.

THE PRESS AND PARLIAMENT

W. T. Stead was the most famous journalist of the 1880s. As editor of the Darlington-based *Northern Echo* in the seventies, his fiery polemic attracted the attention of Gladstone and other leading Liberals. They persuaded Stead to move to London to edit the influential evening paper, the *Pall Mall Gazette*. Stead was the pioneer of sensationalist investigative journalism. He used the *Pall Mall Gazette* to mount a series of campaigns, the most notorious of which was when he went underground to expose the extent of child prostitution and the white slave trade. His reports shocked and scandalised Victorian Britain. W. H. Smith refused to stock the paper during the week Stead's articles were published. But the resulting furore

---

46   Minutes of the Basingstoke Petty Court, 1881–3 and *Hants and Berks Gazette*, 5 November 1881.

47   *Hants and Berks Gazette*, 11 June 1881.

W. T Stead (Author's collections)

persuaded Parliament to raise the age of consent from 13 to 16.[48] In his attempts to publicise the conditions of the poor, he often worked hand in glove with William Booth and other leaders of the Salvation Army. On hearing about the riots of 20 March, probably direct from Booth, Stead travelled down to Basingstoke on the 27th to see for himself.

Stead's report in the *Pall Mall Gazette* on 28 March 1881 drew the events in Basingstoke to the country's attention. Although the events he witnessed have been described already, it is interesting to see how he put it. His description of the morning's procession, though disapproving, shows what fun the Massagainians and their supporters must have had:

> Every contrivance which the ingenuity of the country bumpkins could suggest was employed to make a horrible discord. One man blew long blasts on a huge trombone, another clashed together as cymbals two tin pan lids, a dozen played different tunes on as many tin whistles, one made hideous noises with a clarinet, and another rattled stones in the inside of a tin can. Those without instruments set up discordant howls and yells as they marched through the market-place amid the laughter and jeers of the groups gathered round.

---

48   Clarke, Bob, *From Grub Street to Fleet Street* (Ashgate, 2004; Revel Barker, 2010).

As for the events of that afternoon, Stead continued:

> On came the roughs clashing their cans and brandishing their sticks.
> They passed the 'Salvation Factory', but instead of proceeding along
> the street, they at once turned round and marched backwards and
> forwards immediately in front of the building so the Salvationists
> could not possibly begin their march. For twenty minutes this
> disorderly horde of vagabonds marched backwards and forwards
> under the eyes of the Mayor and the Specials, absolutely nothing
> being done, no attempt whatever being made to abate the nuisance
> or to allow the Army an opportunity of forming in the street. The
> thing was growing monotonous, when one of the roughs pushed
> another against the Captain of the Army, who was immediately
> seized by the Specials. As he shook himself loose, the police
> made a rush to the spot, crying 'Violence' and the Mayor there
> and then, amid the jostling crowd, read the Riot Act . . .[when he
> had finished]. . . the mob sang a stave of 'Rule Britannia' and the
> Specials exhorted one and all to clear the streets. The Salvationists
> at once entered the building. The roughs, having achieved their
> purpose of 'arranging' a disturbance sufficient to afford a pretext
> for reading the Riot Act and preventing the Salvation Army from
> processing the streets, desisted from their clamour; and for the next
> hour Basingstoke was moved to fits of contemptuous laughter by
> watching the attempts of the special constables to clear the streets.
> Twenty mounted artillerymen rode hither and thither, and about
> forty others on foot marched backwards and forwards, driving the
> crowd before them . . . and the streets gradually cleared.

Stead's report was followed up by the *Daily News* and the *Evening
Standard* the following day, and by the *Spectator* (then, a newspaper) and
the *Saturday Review* on 2 April.

On 28 March a deputation of Magistrates visited the Home Office to
discuss the troubles during the past two Sundays and to seek advice on how
to handle future events. Sir William Harcourt, the Home Secretary, asked
the Borough Magistrates for a written report on the disturbances.

The following day in the House of Commons, J C M'Coan, the Member
for Wicklow, asked the Home Secretary:

> Whether his attention had been directed to the report in the *Pall
> Mall Gazette* of March 28th, of a riot which took place on Sunday
> at Basingstoke; and, whether he will take any steps to prevent the
> threatened recurrence of a similar scene on Sunday next?

To which the Home Secretary replied:

The circumstances of this scandalous transaction have been drawn to my notice and I am awaiting a further report on this matter. Everything that I can do will be done to prevent the recurrence of a similar scene next Sunday.[49]

Also on the 29th, F. S. Chandler, the Clerk to the Justices of the Borough of Basingstoke, sent Sir William Harcourt the report he requested:

For the past six months, or thereabouts, a number of persons, styling themselves the Salvation Army, have been in the habit of parading the streets of the town and singing hymns on their way. Their usual course on week-days is to assemble in the market-place about 7 p.m., and, after holding a short service, to proceed four abreast to their place of worship, which is situate on the outskirts of the town. On Sundays they usually hold three such services in the market-place, and walk to and from their place of worship as before mentioned. They appear to use their best endeavours not to block up or stop in any way the streets, but march on the left hand side of the road.

For some weeks past a feeling of opposition to these open air services and processions seems to have arisen, and the Salvation Army have been considerably annoyed and interfered with by a crowd of men and boys.

Several persons have been punished severely for creating disturbances within the meeting house of the Salvation Army. About 17th inst. An anonymous bill, calling upon persons to assemble in the market-place the following Sunday, was circulated. On the morning of Sunday, the 20th day of March inst., the Salvation Army was proceeding, as usual, along the street, singing hymns and carrying at their head a banner or flag.

When they arrived at the junction of Church-street and Cross-street, a considerable crowd of persons, carrying a flag at their head, was observed coming down Church-street. The Salvation Army, in order, it is supposed, not to come into collision with this crowd, turned up Cross-street, and proceeded from thence up New-street. When about half way up the street, they came into collision with the crowd, who seemed to have turned back from Church-street, and proceeded down Winchester-street and New-street, for the purpose of meeting the Army. A good deal of pushing and hustling took place, and the flags of both parties were broken and torn, and the Army, after a great deal of struggling and pushing, succeeded in reaching their place of worship. In the afternoon, the Army again

---

49   House of Commons Debates 29 March 1881 vol. 260 col.155.

proceeded from their place of worship up Church-street, intending, it is supposed, to proceed to the market-place, but when near the Church, a large crowd with a flag at their head, shouting and making a great noise, was perceived coming towards them. To prevent a collision, the leader of the Salvation Army turned into Church-square. The crowd immediately rushed on the Army and broke up their ranks. The Army then formed a ring on the grass plot in the centre of the square, and commenced singing a hymn, but the crowd rushed upon them and broke up the ring, and fighting took place in all directions, and a most riotous disturbance ensued. One man's arm was broken, and a considerable number of the Salvation Army and their partisans, and other persons, received bruises and cuts about the head and face. The mayor of the town was present, and, together with the police, did all in their power to restore order, and were eventually successful in so doing, and the crowd dispersed. It is estimated that quite 3,000 persons were present, although comparatively a small number only took part in the affray. No arrests were made by the police, and no informations were laid or summonses issued with respect to the disturbances.

During the ensuing week the Salvation Army confined themselves to their place of worship, and did not parade the streets, but stated their intention of doing so on the following Sunday, the 27th inst.

The magistrates of the town, fearing that a most serious disturbance and riot would be the consequence, issued summonses to 100 of the principal tradesmen and inhabitants of the town to attend and be sworn in as special constables, and also called out the 16 constables who were appointed for the year in October last. On Sunday morning last, half an hour previous to the time when it was expected the Salvation Army would leave their place of worship and parade the town, the special constables assembled at the Town Hall, and, shortly afterwards, a large crowd of men and boys proceeded down Church-street in the direction of the place of worship of the Salvation Army. The police and special constables, under the direction of the superintendent of police, followed, and were drawn up at the bottom of Church-street.

The Salvation Army presently made its appearance, marching four abreast, and singing a hymn as usual. A portion of the constables were stationed in front of the Army, and the remainder at the rear, and thus escorted, the Army marched round the town, an immense crowd of people following, some of whom were blowing horns and whistle pipes, shouting, and making a great noise.

No violence, however, was used.

After the Army had reached their place of worship about three-fourths of the special constables interviewed the mayor, and protested against being required to escort and protect the Salvation Army, and some of them actually refused to do so.

The mayor, however, fearing a great disturbance in the afternoon, prevailed on them to obey the directions of the superintendent of police for that day, and informed them the magistrates would consider any objection or protest they pleased to make on the morrow.

Shortly before two o'clock, the hour when it was expected the Army would again parade the town, a great crowd of persons appeared in the market-place, with a number of persons at their head, blowing old brass instruments, foghorns, whistles, &c.

They proceeded to the place of worship of the Army, and the constables, under the direction of the superintendent, as before, followed.

The Army came out of their building, and walked in procession some 100 yards along the road, but seeing such a large crowd of people approaching them, returned to their building and posted themselves on the outside of it, leaving, however, ample space for the crowd to go by, and the persons before-mentioned, who were blowing the brass instruments, &c., marched up and down the road, in front of the building.

A great deal of hustling and pushing took place, and it is reported that some of the crowd laid hands on a Mr Jordan, one of the leaders of the Army. The superintendent then called to the mayor, who was present, that there was fighting going on all around him, and requested him (the mayor) to read the Riot Act. The mayor did so, and fearing a general riot, and also believing that the majority of the special constables would sympathise with the crowd, sent a request to the commanding officer of a battery of artillery then staying in the town, en route from Christchurch to London, that he would call out a sufficient number of his men to assist the police in dispersing the mob and clearing the streets.

After some difficulty, and at the expiration of about an hour from the reading of the Riot Act, order was restored. There is no doubt that there is an organised opposition to the Salvation Army, and that it is being conducted under the guidance and direction of some few persons of good average position in the town.

It should be mentioned that the magistrates discovered some bills to be printed, similar to those issued at Salisbury,[50] with references to

---

50   In February 1881 the Home Secretary advised the mayor of Salisbury that if he 'anticipated a riot in consequence of the foolish conduct of a body of persons . . . parading the town in procession', such processions should be banned.

the disturbances in that City, but they were not issued. An interview took place with a so-called captain of the Army, at which interview offers of private meadows were made, in which the members of the Army could meet, and this person said he thought that would meet the difficulty. The offer of the meadows was afterwards refused, in consequence of orders received by the Salvation Army from their headquarters. The magistrates of the town are most anxious to prevent any repetition of such proceedings, but feel assured that so long as the Salvation Army parades the streets there will be a large number of persons who will endeavour to oppose the Army, and that most serious riots and disturbances will be the probable result.

They are, therefore, desirous of ascertaining what steps should be taken on their part to prevent such proceedings in the future, and in the event of their believing it desirable to issue similar proclamations to those issued at Salisbury, their course, in case the Salvation Army parades the streets as heretofore in defiance of such proclamation.[51]

On 1 April 1881 the Home Office replied, echoing the advice given to the Liverpool magistrates in 1865 concerning violence associated with Orange parades, that, while such processions were not illegal in themselves, if they were likely to 'lead to riotous collision' and endanger the peace of the town, the magistrates should issue notices banning the processions. If, despite this, the Salvation Army gave notice that they intended to go ahead with their procession, the magistrates should get assistance from the County Police and swear in special constables to stop the procession forming and disperse any crowd that gathered with the intention of interfering with the procession.

The Home Office's advice appears to have been delivered by messenger, for on the same day (1 April) the magistrates issued a proclamation forbidding all processions and open air gatherings.

General Booth complained to the Home Office that the magistrates' proclamation was unlawful. He said the Army would hold a procession, as they could not relinquish their rights as citizens to hold public meetings in the open spaces and streets of this country:

> The magistrates have given us to understand that we shall get no protection from the mob on Sunday, and the special constables who have already been sworn in and armed with truncheons will be left to join the rabble in attacking our people and doing what they say they will do, 'break their heads' . . . The magistrates yesterday further showed their animus by refusing to grant summonses against sixteen rioters unless they had written information in every case signed by a responsible person, thus delaying as long as possible our attempt

51   Parliamentary Papers (1882) Cmd, 132, vol. 54.

to bring these persons to justice, and giving the opportunities to the others to hatch up cases against us.[52]

The Home Office replied to General Booth that they noted that the Salvation Army intended to disregard the proclamation in order to test the law, but that the Secretary of State, 'thinks it needless for him to point out to you the serious character of this determination', but if they were planning to go ahead, they should warn the magistrates so that, on the appearance of their procession, the magistrates 'may take such steps as they deem fit to enforce their proclamation; thus avoiding any subsequent riot or breach of the peace'. The Home Office copied this correspondence to Mayor Blatch.

Blatch reported back to the Home Secretary that the leaders of the Salvation Army with Mr Barron, had called on him to say that they intended to hold a procession as a test case only, and that they would halt their procession if the police forced them to stop. They attempted a procession, but the police stopped them and they retired back to the barracks, 'and our town has been, I am thankful to say, as quiet, if not more so, than usual.'[53]

The Salvation Army did not get the test case it wanted, as the police refused to arrest anyone. They did, however, do their best to try to get arrested, and thus be able to test the legality of the proclamation and the Home Secretary's instructions. Superintendent Rapkins of the County Police complained that the Salvationists stamped on his toes and those of his constables in an attempt to be arrested.

After the proclamation banning street processions was issued, many of the pubs displayed Union Jacks from their upper windows. In the evening of Tuesday 5 April, Councillor Tubb hosted a supper for the Massagainians, where £15 was collected 'to meet Massagainian expenses'.[54] The fund raising continued: the *Gazette*, in a leader column on 16 April said,

> The Massagainians are still alive and are ready for mischief. On Wednesday evening they were sending round the hat to certain publicans for subscriptions. A Town Councillor is reported to have contributed a sovereign, others smaller sums, to put the Army down.

Later, at a Town Council meeting, Councillor John May, the brewer and town benefactor, complained that Councillor Schofield had been telling people that he (Councillor May) had given £5 to the Massaganians to support them against the Salvation Army. He said that people must think him very simple if they really believed that he had thus supported the

---

52   Ibid.
53   Parliamentary Papers (1882) Cmd, 132, vol. 54.
54   *Hants and Berks Gazette*, 9 April 1881.

Massagainians in flying in the face of the magistrates. Schofield admitted he had made the statement, but said he had got that information from a reliable source.[55]

Because the police did not charge anybody in connection with the 20 March riot, the Salvation Army took out summonses against some of the Massagainians. The Massaganians took out counter-summonses for assault against some of Salvation Army supporters, including the Wallises. Hearings took place on 5 and 11 April, mainly in respect of the counter-summonses against the Salvation Army supporters. Of the few cases that were heard, the magistrates dismissed the charges on the grounds that the blows were struck in the confusion of a general row between two opposing groups. The solicitors for both sides responded by withdrawing the remaining summonses.

However, it appears that the Salvation Army changed its mind. It took out fresh summonses in the name of Edward Clayton. These were heard on 3 and 9 May before Mayor Blatch, ex-Mayor Allen, Henry Portsmouth and Richard Knight:

> Edward Adams, Charles Adams and Valentine Adams, brewers, Frank Barkham, painter, Harry Barkham, coach painter, George Rose, seed merchant's foreman, Frank Powell, labourer, Albert Lansley, blacksmith, Thomas Emery, labourer, Daniel Hatton, labourer, Ernest Fitzgerald, hawker and Frank Chalk, stonemason, were charged by Edward Clayton, platelayer, that they, on the 20th March, with force of arms, unlawfully and riotously, did assemble and gather together to disturb the peace of our Lady the Queen. They were also charged with assaulting Edward Clayton, William Hudson, John Fennell, Charles Elms, George Collins, George Doswell and others; and also with creating a great disturbance, to the terror of the liege subjects of the Queen.[56]

After the last witness for the Salvation Army had been heard, Mr Bullen, the barrister representing the Massaganians, addressed the magistrates:

> The charge is that a body of men had organised a state of terrorism in this town which had resulted in riot and assault, but when one comes to look at the state of affairs in Basingstoke, one cannot help thinking that the odium which has been brought upon the town is not to be attributed to the peace-loving regular inhabitants but by the Army itself. By their so-called Christianity, they outraged the feelings of many; and they still continued that practice, which must lead to a breach of the peace. Persons are no doubt entitled

---

55   Town Council meeting, 4 August 1881.
56   Report of the Proceedings before the Magistrates, on 3 and 9 May, 1881 (no publisher noted).

to express their opinions, and also to give outward expressions to
those opinions, but not when they lead to tumult and disorder . . .
Until this body known as the Salvation Army was formed here,
the number of summonses which came before the Magistrates was
comparatively unknown. They now had a large number of assault
cases to hear. Prior to the 20th March there had been disturbances.
The Army knew perfectly well that their conduct was leading to
disturbances in the town. A counter demonstration was made by
people who resisted the thrusting of religious views upon them . . .
[but] they were not headed by a flag bearing the words 'Blood and
Fire' (which to some persons is a sort of challenge), but simply the
Union Jack. They met the Army; and upon that, one of the more
muscular Salvationists – Mr Elms – gave the signal for war by
seizing the flag, and so created the disturbance.[57]

He said the evidence from the witnesses who had appeared was
untrustworthy. He asked why the prosecution had not put the Wallises,
'gentlemen far superior to some of the witnesses who had been called', in
the witness box as it was claimed they had been assaulted. If they had been
he would have got out in cross-examination 'how far they were a party to
this matter, how far they were lending their help, and how far they were the
instigators of this affair.' He also suggested that the prosecution had not
dared to put 'the two reverend gentlemen', Mr Trevethick and Mr Barron,
in the box. If they had, the court would 'no doubt have got at the truth'.
He asked whether it was right for the prosecution to withhold from the
magistrates the only reliable evidence. When he had finished his speech,
'there was much applause'.

The magistrates retired to consider their verdict. When they returned,
Mayor Blatch said they had come to the conclusion that there was not
sufficient evidence to justify sending the case for trial, and consequently the
defendants would be dismissed.

Mr Bullen then said that even the Salvation Army might learn a lesson
from their opponents. He was instructed by the defendants, for the sake of
peace and quietness, to do what the Army refused to do, that is, withdraw
the summonses taken out against the Army's supporters.

When Mr Bullen left the court with the defendants, he was 'heartily
cheered' by the crowd waiting outside the courtroom. When Henry Barron
and the Salvationists left the court, they were 'greeted with groans, hisses
and other manifestations of disapprobation.'[58]

---

57   Ibid.
58   *Hants and Berks Gazette*, 14 May 1881.

THE TOWN AND MAGISTRATES DIVIDED

The report in the *Hants and Berks Gazette* for 9 April 1881, under the heading, 'Basingstoke Town Council – Heated Discussion', showed that the Council was divided between those who supported the rights of the Salvation Army to hold processions and services in the streets, and those who were against. Here is an extract:

> *Councillor [George] Dunn* – I would like to ask you [Blatch] as Mayor and chief magistrate of this town, who is responsible for instructions given to the police for the protection of Her Majesty's subjects in the public streets . . . I know for a fact that some of Her Majesty's subjects in this town have gone in fear of their lives. Assaults have been committed openly, and the police have not taken the people who committed those assaults in charge . . . The law has been trampled under foot, and we have been under mob rule . . . I think it is a question that the magistrates should take up.
>
> *Alderman Henry Portsmouth* – As one of the magistrates, I shall have great pleasure in answering that. It has been stated to me that the police have not done their duty in arresting persons that have committed assaults in this town . . . Our clerk says there must be a breach of the peace, and that you must see the blow struck before a man can be arrested. Are you going to take up all?
>
> *Alderman Arthur Wallis* – [referring to 20 March] There must have been a considerable amount of rioting and violence. I was away from home, but three of my sons and a young gentleman were in town and were openly assaulted by the mob. They took no part either one way or the other. One of them had a violent blow in the back, and another was struck in the head. The one that received the blow in the head certainly did turn round and knock the fellow down. How was it that these assaults took place and none of the police saw them?
>
> *Alderman [Henry] Allen* – The conduct of the police has been investigated by the magistrates . . . and I can safely say that the majority of the magistrates were of the opinion that the police had done their duty. It is very well known that Mr Richard Wallis was a great friend to the Salvation Army, to which no one objected,

although at the time things began to look troublesome he placed himself at the head of the Army. But gentlemen, things went on, and although the Salvation Army were here for five or six weeks no disturbance took place, although there may have been a little opposition. But what was the cause of the disturbance in the first place? Simply because Mr Richard Wallis took upon himself to write a letter to the Home Secretary without consulting his brother magistrates, and without bringing before the Watch Committee that the police had not done their duty; and when the letter was brought to the magistrates and was read, the commencement of the letter was, 'As a last resort I appeal to you to protect the Salvation Army', and then further he says, 'I sign this as the senior magistrate. I have spoken to the Superintendent and he tells me he doesn't know which masters to obey.' The consequences of this letter have been to bring him into disrepute and a bill was put out on which were the words, 'Dirty Dick', and he applied this to himself. That was the first commencement of the row, then came the question of political strife, religious and political feud . . . Mr Richard Wallis brought up about the mob trying to rush the young woman into the *Ship*, and said the police did not attempt to protect her. In reply to this Sergeant Waldren said that before there was any disturbance, he went to the young woman and said, 'If you stand by me, I will protect you.' The answer was, her duty was to remain with her Army, and she said, 'I will go with the Army, if I die for it.' What could the sergeant do? He proved to the magistrates that he did all he could to quell the row. What would be the use of eight or ten policemen in the event of three or four hundred people getting together? Are they to reach in and take the first man they see fighting? The facts of the riot in Church-square were clearly stated by Superintendent Hibberd. He said, 'The Army came one way and the mob the other. When I turned round the corner I saw Mr Wallis' sons hitting right and left.' What would Mr Wallis have said if the Superintendent had taken them up?

    Councillor May – Can't the Salvation Army be induced to keep to their place of meeting for a time until this excitement has blown over?

Richard Wallis not only wrote to the Home Secretary behind the backs of the Council and his fellow magistrates, but it appears that he also wrote to the Lord Chancellor seeking his approval for John Burgess Soper, Thomas Maton Kingdon, and Arkas Sapp to be appointed as magistrates. It seems the first the Council heard of this was when they received a letter from the Lord Chancellor approving the appointments.

Alderman Portsmouth complained that the nomination of new magistrates was normally made by the Council as a whole – it was not the prerogative of one man to go behind the backs of the Council. He moved a

Left: Henry Allen (Hampshire County Council Museums & Arts Service)
Right: Richard Wallis (Basingstoke & Deane Borough Council)

resolution that the Council felt that those individuals were not qualified to hold the position of Justices of the Peace.

Councillor May said that he:

> . . . was sorry that we have persons who have made themselves so eager for new magistrates. If such a thing was required, it should be done in a fair and open way. Go in the front door; not by the back. Come forward in a straightforward manner, and not go sneaking behind one's back and do an indecency and an injustice to fellow magistrates.

This prompted Richard Wallis to write an indignant letter to the *Gazette*: '. . . as for the brewer's remarks about going to the front and not to the back door, I suppose he considers the brewers' and the publicans' interest the front door.'[59]

Alderman Portsmouth's resolution was seconded by Mayor Blatch and Alderman Allen and was passed. But it was too late: the Lord Chancellor had approved the appointments.

On 27 June 1881 Soper, Kingdon and Sapp took the oath as magistrates at County Hall, Winchester. The following evening, the magistrates met, augmented by the new boys, and, 'after some discussion', resolved to give the police orders not to stop the Salvation Army processions, but that no

---

59   *Hants and Berks Gazette*, 9 April 1881.

notice of the withdrawal of the proclamation of 1 April should be made, and that the police have 'stringent orders to do their best to prevent a breach of the peace.'[60]

'FURTHER MASSAGAINIAN DISTURBANCES'

When the magistrates met the following week, George Greenaway summonsed Richard Sheppard, a shoemaker, for indecent behaviour at the Salvation Army factory on 3 July during the hours of divine worship. Sheppard was with Richard Hatton and Edward Bone. One of them shouted 'Amen in a disgraceful manner', and Sheppard burst out laughing. When a man stood up to say how God had saved his soul, Sheppard called out, 'You're a liar, everyone who says he is saved is a liar, and I can prove it by scripture.'

William Hudson, the teacher of music, complained to the magistrates that he kept being followed by 'the man, Barkham' (presumably Frank), Edward Bone and others, who called him names, and Barkham had 'more than once blown furious blasts in his ear out of a large brass instrument he was in the habit of carrying.'

Despite the *Gazette*'s unwavering support for the Salvation Army and its constant appeals for the magistrates and police to take a tougher line against the Massagainians, it seems that from time to time the writers were reluctantly amused by some of the antics of the Massagainians, and by Frank Barkham in particular. Under the heading, 'Further Massagainian Disturbances' in its issue of 9 July 1881, the *Gazette* described the events surrounding the Salvation Army procession through the town on the evening of Wednesday, 6 July, and gave an almost affectionate portrait of Frank Barkham. Here is an extract:

> The progress of the crowd through Essex-road was slow, and was performed in the greatest confusion. The Army continued their singing with considerable earnestness, and the Massagainians were not at all feeble in their efforts to create as much noise as they could. Our old acquaintance Barkham, by this time well-known to most of our readers, was entrusted with a huge brass instrument which was placed round his shoulders, and into which he blew with all his might, and with startling effect. Another individual, whose visage betokened that he was fresh from some forge, created a horrible sound by turning a large wooden rattle. The tin can was again brought into use while the Massagainian vocalists were untiring in their exertions to instil a little 'harmony' into the music of the Salvationists. The proceedings of both parties, however, appeared to

---

60   Minutes of the Basingstoke Petty Court, 1881–3.

be carried out with the utmost good humour . . . After a short time, during which the Army pressed into their building as quickly as possible, the crowd commenced to disperse, not, however, before a few cheers had been raised on behalf of the Masssagainians. Master Barkham was soon proceeding towards Winchester-street with unmistakable signs of satisfaction on his countenance, and was soon called into a well-known public house, where he was greeted with roars of laughter.

There was trouble when the Salvation Army marched through the town in the evening of 14 July 1881. On their return down Sarum Hill they met a group of Massagainians, including Frank Barkham, Ernest Fitzgerald, Frank Powell, Richard Humphries and George Thompson. When the Army were in procession, Frank Barkham's technique was to try to separate the ranks by barging into them with his elbows out, claiming they were obstructing the highway, and then running back in front of them to repeat the performance. Either that, or marching with his mates in front of the procession making farting noises with his brass instrument to drown out the hymns, and suddenly stopping from time to time. If the procession cannoned into him when he stopped, he would turn round and clout the nearest person.

Frank seems to have left his brass instrument at home that evening, so he adopted his first technique. George Cooke, one of the Army's supporters, complained to the magistrates that Frank kept barging into him with his elbows as they were marching down Sarum Hill. When they reached the *New Inn*, Frank pushed him across the road shouting, 'You bugger, I'll do for you.' He continued to threaten Cooke as they marched down Essex Road. So much so that Cooke said he was afraid to go home and remained with the Army in their barracks. Eventually, when Cooke was walking home, Frank came rushing out of the *Victory Inn* with his baby, Ada, in his arms, shouting at Cooke, 'I'll do for you yet.'

William Newman, another Salvation Army supporter, complained that Frank hit him on the shoulder with his fist as he barged through the procession. Other witnesses complained that when they were trying to sing their hymn, Frank kept howling 'like a madman'.

The magistrates convicted Frank for both assaults, fining him £1 8s 0d plus 12 shillings costs for the George Cooke offence and £1 10s 0d plus 10 shillings cost for hitting William Newman. Frank was given 14 days to pay, or one month in prison if he defaulted.[61]

On the afternoon of Sunday 24 July 1881, while Superintendent Hibberd was on patrol, he heard 'a great noise' in Reading Road. He found

---

61 Minutes of the Basingstoke Petty Court, 1881–3.

'Moses and his followers', as he described Captain Moses and the Salvation Army, trying to hold a service in the chalk dell. A large crowd stood in the road, jeering, and Richard Humphries, William Jones and Thomas Cowdery were ringing bells to disrupt the service. Superintendent Hibberd later told the Court that he spoke to the three bell ringers as loudly as he could, 'You are obstructing the highway here, and annoying parties.' He asked them to move on, which they did only by moving backwards and forwards, still ringing their bells 'for some considerable time', before moving off to *The Old House At Home* to quench their thirst while lying in wait for the Salvation Army to finish their service.

When the Salvation Army reached Brook Street on their way back from the Dell a crowd of some 500 people surrounded them, including the three bell ringers. The procession had come to a halt because Spencer Doman, Robert Duke and John Hunt were standing in front, leaning back against the Salvation Army with all their strength, blocking their way. When the police asked them to move on, they did so, but very slowly, taking steps of about five or six inches at a time and stopping every five or six yards. When Sergeant Waldren remonstrated with them, Doman said that he had as much right to the road as the others.

When the case came to court the six defendants were charged with 'unlawfully and wilfully obstructing the free passage of a certain highway named Brook-street by then and there assembling to the number of 500 persons or thereabout.' Thomas Newman appeared for the defendants and told the court:

> If the Salvation Army went shouting and bawling through the streets they must expect to meet with ridicule. They had no more right to go bawling through the street than did his clients who went about with their bells.

The magistrates found the six defendants guilty and fined them five shillings each, plus 2s 2d costs, or seven days in jail in default of payment.[62]

The following Sunday, 31 July 1881, John Clark, by now an unemployed solicitor's clerk, attacked Captain Moses as he was leading a procession past the *Wheatsheaf*. Moses brought a prosecution before the borough magistrates on 9 August, stating that Clark had rushed across the road and barged into him with his shoulder. Clark repeated this twice more and then trod on Moses's foot in an attempt to trip him up. Clark was fined £2 with 10s 6d costs and given 24 hours to pay, with one month's hard labour in default.[63]

---

62   Ibid.
63   Ibid.

THE TWO PETITIONS

Blatch and Richard Knight visited the Home Office on 10 August 1881. Blatch told the Home Office that, as a result of the appointment of the new magistrates, he was no longer supported by the majority on the bench in his attempts to carry out the instructions the Home Secretary sent him in April to prevent the Salvation Army processions. Before the new magistrates were appointed, the proclamation was successfully enforced. But for the last few weeks, the Army had been allowed to march through the town again, 'and the result has been a great amount of disturbance, to the annoyance of all quietly disposed persons.' Blatch said that he wanted to prevent their processions and their singing through the streets, which was the primary cause of the disturbances. He feared that there would be the most serious results unless the processions were stopped. It seemed hard that he, as Mayor, should be held responsible for consequences he could easily prevent if he was still able to carry out the Home Secretary's directions. A few weeks before, the magistrates told the police not to break up the Salvation Army's processions. This was done as an experiment, but in his view the experiment had failed.[64]

Blatch also sent the Home Secretary a petition that was presented to the mayor and magistrates by Thomas Pain of Audley House. It was signed by James Elwin Millard, the Vicar of Basingstoke and 498 others, including those who styled themselves 'Gentlemen', such as Thomas Pain and Samuel Field of Goldings, 'Independent Ladies', including the two Miss Simmons from Highfield House, professional men (clergymen, solicitors, architects, surveyors, surgeons, bank managers, schoolmasters, etc.), corn and timber merchants, farmers, shopkeepers (ironmongers, drapers, stationers, etc.), as well as brewers (Mayor Blatch's two sons and Harry Loe, Barratt's brewery manager), publicans, plumbers, bricklayers, painters and labourers, including Frank and Harry Barkham and other Massagainians.[65] It read:

> We, the undersigned residents and ratepayers of the town of
> Basingstoke . . . assure you that we deeply deplore the sad scenes of
> riot and discord which have taken place in the streets of our town
> in connection with what is called the Salvation Army, and which
> desecrates our Christian Sabbath and caused the greatest pain and
> discomfort to hundreds of Christian persons who desire to worship
> God in the quiet manner to which they have been accustomed.
>
> We had hoped that as the steps so prudently taken . . . to prevent
> these processions in the public streets on account of the danger, riot

---

64   Parliamentary Papers (1882) Cmd, 132, vol. 54.
65   TNA PRO HO 45/9607/A2886.

Henry Barron (London Street Congregational Church; photo Robert Applin)

and disorder connected therewith, would be strictly and persistently carried out, because the manifest quiet thereby has been so truly appreciated by the inhabitants of the town.

But from present appearances we fear that you are rather disposed to depart from those steps, and to permit such public processions to be renewed notwithstanding the painful remembrance of such deplorable scenes which took place in the past.

We do, therefore, venture to entreat and urge you to continue the prohibition of such in the public streets because of the danger unavoidably connected therewith.[66]

Not to be outflanked, the five nonconformist Magistrates – Richard Wallis, Arthur Wallis, Thomas Maton Kingdon, Arkas Sapp and John Burgess Soper – instructed the Clerk to the Borough Justices to send a rival petition to the Home Secretary. This was signed by Henry Barron and 613 others, including John Bird of the *Hants and Berks Gazette*:

We, the undersigned burgesses, ratepayers, and other inhabitants of the town of Basingstoke, beg respectfully to address you in reference to the continued opposition to, and annoyance of, the Salvation Army on the part of an organised band, promoted and supported by those who are interested in preventing their work . . . the said Army has been the means . . . of raising persons of low, immoral, and drunken habits, to paths of virtue, sobriety and religion, they

66   Parliamentary Papers (1882) Cmd, 132, vol. 54.

are deserving of all legal protection and support . . . any temporary annoyance which may be felt on the part of those to whom their singing and marching through the streets are repugnant, is amply counterbalanced by the great good they have been the means of doing . . . the unseemly noise and confusion are created by persons in the employ of those interested in hindering the work of the Army . . . for the avowed purpose of bringing the Army into disrepute and odium, and to allow those tactics to succeed, would . . . give a power to the lowest and most unscrupulous persons.

The petition went on to request that the Salvation Army be permitted to parade the streets twice on a Sunday and two or three times during the week and to be given the fullest protection.[67]

Unfortunately, only the first page of this petition has survived. I think the petition started out with the congregation of the London Street Congregational Church before spreading further afield. I have no reason to suggest that this petition did not also cut across the same class and occupational lines as the opposing petition. In both cases the petitions contained the signatures of town councillors.

The five nonconformist magistrates also wrote to the Home Secretary. They said that the Salvation Army's processions and singing had:

. . . succeeded in reclaiming many immoral persons beyond the reach of ordinary evangelistic effort . . . when the effects of their work began to appear in empty public-houses . . . disorderly classes employed, as we have reason to believe, by persons interested in the drink trade, began to create disturbances with a view of preventing the Salvation Army making their way through the streets.

It is our opinion that if the mayor, who is the largest brewer in the town, and the whole bench of magistrates, had acted with energy and firmness at the beginning, these disturbances would have been speedily quelled; but by vacillation and indecision in dealing with the cases of assault that were brought before them by the Salvation Army, the rioters were encouraged, and consequently the disturbances greatly increased. . .

At the beginning of last April the mayor, acting, as he said, under your orders, issued a proclamation forbidding the Salvation Army and other denominations to procession [*sic*] the streets or hold any open-air meetings for the future. The Nonconformists of the town loudly and unanimously protested against this prohibitory bill as a violation of a liberty enjoyed for many generations by every body of Christians; and in conjunction with the Salvation Army gave

---

67   Ibid.

notice to the authorities that they would test its legality, by breaking it. No proceedings were taken against them . . . the conclusion arrived at was that there was no legality in it. The street processions have therefore continued until the present time, and so have the disturbances.

The mayor and Mr Knight desire to reissue the proclamation, but we, being the majority of the magistrates (five to two), have a strong objection to such a procedure, regarding it as unnecessary to restore peace and order to the town, and, in our opinion, would be an interference with liberty.

The letter went on to say that the Salvation Army were not responsible for 'the disgraceful proceedings'. The entire blame lay with:

. . . an organised band of roughs, who are, we believe, the paid agents of persons connected with the liquor traffic in the town, whose aim is, by marching in front and at the sides of the Army, making discordant noises, beating old kettles, trays, &c., and blowing horns, to bring that body into odium and disrepute.

They asked whether the police could summon and arrest the roughs for their conduct, and whether they could take proceedings against their employers if they could obtain sufficient evidence to incriminate them.[68]

The Home Office replied on 19 August that they could not advise on legal questions as they depended on the facts of each case as they arose. The Home Secretary could only refer the magistrates to the advice in the letter of 1 April, which seemed to have put an end to the serious riots. The magistrates were responsible for preserving the peace of the town, and it was their duty to take measures to prevent any proceedings which were likely to cause disorder.[69]

As Sir William Harcourt pointed out in another context, the Government was not the keeper of the peace. Keeping the peace was entrusted to the magistrates in the localities for which they had jurisdiction. The Government and the Home Secretary had no authority to give any orders to the magistrates and had no authority over the local police. That being the case, the magistrates who had the knowledge of the state of affairs in a district had the responsibility for dealing with it and the authority to do so. They could seek the advice of the Home Secretary (as the Basingstoke magistrates had done), but the magistrates were not bound by it, and had to use their own discretion based on their local knowledge.[70]

On 23 August the magistrates met for a special meeting. Knight did not

68   Ibid.
69   Ibid.
70   House of Commons Debates, 14 July 1884, vol. 290, col.1120.

turn up, and Blatch, who wished to distance himself from what the other magistrates were about to do, vacated the chair, leaving Richard Wallis to preside. The remaining magistrates, the five who had written to the Home Secretary, passed a resolution that Superintendent Hibberd should tell Captain Moses that if the Army came out in procession once on a Sunday morning and twice in the week only, one or more police constables would go with them. The magistrates also passed a resolution that the Mayor and the Corporation should consider the practicalities of passing a bye-law to afford proper protection to the Salvation Army.[71]

Blatch vented his displeasure by writing to the Home Secretary:

> The magistrates met here yesterday, and the superintendent of police declared himself ready to swear an information that if the Salvation Army were allowed to procession [sic], a disturbance of a serious character would follow. I thereupon proposed that the proclamation that we were advised to issue in April should be again resorted to; but I was outvoted . . . after which I left the chair and the meeting. They then resolved that the Salvation Army should be specially protected round the town on certain days only. This evening was the first attempt and the result has been the worst disturbance we have had for a long time. I am now utterly unable to act, being outvoted, and cannot answer for any consequences unless these processions are put a stop to.[72]

The Home Office sent a brief acknowledgement in reply.

The Town Council met on 2 September to consider the magistrates' request for a new bye-law. Mayor Blatch said the object was to enable the authorities to take more stringent steps to put down anything in opposition to the Salvation Army.

Councillor Webb said, 'Then I think we ought to begin at the beginning and stop the Salvation Army. They are the cause of all this disturbance, and they do it under the garb of religion . . . They say that in order to be known they must go about the streets. They have become well known now I'm sure, and as they have their regular established place of worship, let them stay there, and then those who wish to go to them can do so. They know full well that the others will oppose them, and I really don't see any difference between them, and the result is a disturbance.'

Councillor Poulter said that he agreed with Councillor Webb. He considered both parties to blame, but that the disturbances arose in the first place from the Salvation Army, 'They ought to be obliged to stay in their own house. I have never heard of such disturbances in all my life as we have

71   Minutes of the Basingstoke Petty Court, 1881–3.
72   Parliamentary Papers (1882) Cmd, 132, vol. 54.

Arthur Wallis (Basingstoke & Deane Borough Council)

been having in our midst lately, and we ought to do something to put them down'.

Councillor Dunn responded, 'This is a question of religious persecution . . . [Jesus] . . . was met with the same abuse as the Salvation Army are now receiving in Basingstoke, as were Whitfield and Wesley . . . The respectable people do not come out and annoy them as in Wesley's time, but what do they do? They put the power in the hands of some of the most wretched and drunken characters possible, whom we see constantly reeling about our streets, disturbing the inhabitants of the town . . . I persist that the cause of the disturbances is not the Salvation Army. You cannot stop the processions legally, and there is no law in the land that will take away their liberty.'

Mayor Blatch said that the proclamation of 1 April followed the advice he received from the Home Secretary, 'and it was a most successful course so long as I was supported by my fellow magistrates. After the appointment of three new magistrates, they turned against me instead of acting upon the advice I was acting upon, and the result you see. The course I took I thought to be the best one to bring about a better feeling in the town. I have not, in any shape or form, shown any favouritism towards either party, and the peace of the town has caused me the greatest anxiety and worry.'

Arthur Wallis said he disagreed with the Mayor, 'Seeing that processions are legal, the authorities must use every means in their power to maintain their legality. Last week I was in Birmingham, and there I found that these people came out without being interfered with, even in that large and thickly populated town.'

He was supported by the excitable Councillor Schofield, who said, 'This is a question of religious liberty, and on that ground I shall maintain it . . . for the last four years I have observed that as soon as a man has been elected Mayor of this town, so soon [*sic*] as he has ceased to act with reason and common sense, and that is the cause of the disturbances!'

Mayor Blatch told him that he had a happy knack of saying things that were not true and then retracting, 'I think it would be as well not to say them at all.'

'I don't want to be interrupted,' Councillor Schofield shouted, 'The Salvation Army has nothing to do with the disturbances. They will civilise and reform the country, and I know for a fact that many homes have changed from misery to happiness through these people, and that is why I will ever stand up for them.'

Councillors Schofield and Tubb then got into a slanging match. As there was no consensus, it was decided to defer a decision to a meeting of the Watch Committee the following Thursday.

THE WATCH COMMITTEE VERSUS THE MAGISTRATES[73]

The Watch Committee met on Thursday, 8 September. Mayor Blatch opened the proceedings by saying, 'I think in times like these . . . of riot and disorder, it is as well that a meeting should be called, because we are all interested in restoring peace and order to our streets. I am sorry we have a difference of opinion on the bench. We should all unite in doing our very best, calmly and deliberately, to see if we cannot bring our town into a proper state of quietness.'

Alderman Allen asked Superintendent Hibberd whether he was prepared to swear that riots were more likely if the processions were still persisted in. Superintendent Hibberd confirmed that he was. Alderman Allen then said, 'No one can dispute the fact that the town has been held up to ridicule . . . The time has arisen when the magistrates have shown their incapacity to act from the fact of asking us to make a bye-law . . . A great calamity has fallen upon the town of Basingstoke; you have had your Sabbaths desecrated . . . How is this to be remedied? I shall propose that the Mayor be requested to take such steps as he may think expedient to prevent any further breaches of the peace, and in so doing, His Worship be requested to follow as nearly as possible the instructions received from the Home Office.'

Councillor Webb agreed, 'We have gone to the proper authority, and we are told what to do. Stop the processions and the whole disorder is stopped. The Superintendent says he is prepared to swear on oath that a riot will take place if these people are allowed to come out.'

---

73   Headline in the *Hants and Berks Gazette*, 10 September 1881.

Councillor Dunn countered that the Watch Committee had no power to do what Alderman Allen suggested, 'The resolution means that we are to take the governing of the town into our own hands, and this we cannot do.'

Councillor Smith told the Mayor, 'I don't think we are called here to censure the magistrates . . . you have issued the proclamation, and it has not been withdrawn. You issued it, but did not act upon it, and therefore I say it is ridiculous to make another.'

The Mayor replied, 'I think Mr Smith is acquainted with only part of the facts of the case. At the time the proclamation was issued, it was acted upon, and during this time, week by week the disturbances grew less and less, and I firmly believe that if we had acted upon the same course throughout, we should have cured this evil . . . but a time arrived when three more gentlemen were placed upon the bench of magistrates . . . the results of their appointment was that the Salvation Army came out immediately it was known, in force, and the consequences have been riot and confusion ever since, growing worse and worse.'

Councillor Follett said he had great pleasure supporting the proposition, 'I hear that that the Captain of the Army and the Captain of the Massagainians shake hands before and after the processions, and if the opposing force is there first, Captain Moses says, 'Oh, where's Barkham? Here you must wait a few minutes as we are not ready.'

Alderman Allen's proposition was put to the vote, and was supported by all, except Councillors Smith and Dunn, who were greeted with ironical laughter when the 'noes' were called for.[74]

CHURCH VERSUS DISSENT

Relations between the religious organisations in Basingstoke appear to have been amicable. The denominations might have had their differences on doctrinal matters, but they tended to work together for the common good on school and charitable boards, for example; and Canon Millard worked alongside the Congregationalists as a Director of the Old Angel Café Company. However, the coming of the Salvation Army polarised opinion between Church and Dissent. We have already seen the very active support and encouragement the nonconformist denominations gave to the Salvation Army. The Church of England in Basingstoke took a completely different line, as can be seen from these extracts from the *Basingstoke Parish Magazine*:

> Nearly a year has passed since the association which claims this title [the Salvation Army] 'opened fire', to use their own phrase, on this town. It is not premature to attempt something like a summing up

---

74   *Hants and Berks Gazette*, 10 September 1881.

of the results of this campaign. We are told that great numbers have been reformed and converted. To ordinary eyes the apparent change in this place shows itself in perpetual disorder, bitter quarrels, a defiance of all authority, a steady decline in good discipline and government, noisy irreverent assemblages on the Lord's Day, and religion passing into a standing joke.[75]

It is impossible to deny that there has been, during the last 12 months, a visible falling off in the moral tone of the place. And for much of that we do not hesitate to say the 'Salvation Army' is responsible. Of course its promoters intended something very different. Perhaps their eccentric movements have, in some instances, brought drunkards or profligates to a better mind. On this point there is much difference of opinion and little satisfactory evidence . . . Can they be blind to the fact that the opposition which they have stirred up, is filling the public houses as they have never been filled before? . . . [The Salvation Army has] an arrogant disregard for their neighbours' comfort and convenience.[76]

The *Hampshire Chronicle* printed a letter on 24 September 1881, saying:

The protracted nuisance occasioned by the so-called Salvation Army which has rendered the ordinary business of life so uncomfortable by the 'army's' interference . . . appears to me to demand sharp and prompt action on the part of the law. The peaceful inhabitants and traders have been studiously annoyed, and the public quiet needlessly interrupted by gangs of so-called missionaries with obscure, but all the more noisy 'leaders' of both sexes . . . I think we may assume that Christianity has little to gain from their excursions and al-fresco hallelujahs.

Opinion in the town was divided as never before.

75 Basingstoke Parish Magazine, September 1881.
76 Ibid, October 1881.

THE MASSAGAINIAN MARTYRS

It may be safely affirmed that when the carriage which conveyed the prisoners pulled out of Basingstoke Station, there died the last hope of popularity for the Salvation Army.

Hampshire Chronicle, 10 September 1881

Tuesday, 30 August 1881 was a particularly busy day for the magistrates and it further demonstrated the split between those magistrates who supported the Salvation Army, and those against. There were four cases concerning disturbances connected with the Salvation Army. They were heard by Mayor Blatch, Richard Knight, Richard and Arthur Wallis, Thomas Maton Kingdon and Arkas Sapp.

The first case concerned a scuffle between Henry Hewitt and Fred Beckett, while the Salvation Army were marching down Church Street. Hewitt told the magistrates:

> I saw Beckett opposite Mr Evans's the Tailor. He looked up to me and said, 'Who are you a-shoving of?' I had not touched him. I said, 'Who are you talking to man, about shoving?' and he replied, 'Who are you talking to?' He then hit me in the mouth with his fist and made my mouth bleed. I was spitting blood for half an hour afterwards.[77]

Henry Hewitt described Fred Beckett as being about 30 years of age. Fred did not appear in court. Instead his mother appeared on his behalf. She explained that Fred could not attend as he was subject to fits, having had five fits since Saturday. Fred was fined 10 shillings plus 9s 6d costs.

The next case was brought by Edwin Andrews and Charles Ford, two Salvationists, who summonsed Richard Humphries for assault. Andrews said that in the evening of 22 August he was marching with the Army down Rayleigh Road when Humphries:

> . . . refused to let me pass that way. I asked why. He there and then pushed me about with his elbows, turning his back to me. He said, 'You knocked my hat off.' I said, 'I've not.' He started pushing again with his hands in front. In his pushing, he fell down. He got up and said, 'You kicked my arse.' I had not kicked him. He tucked up his

77   Minutes of the Basingstoke Petty Court, 1881–3.

shirt sleeves and put his fist in my face. He said, 'I'll knock your bloody head off.' He then struck me on the right side of the face under the eye and then struck me under the jaw. [I said] 'I have not touched you, my good friend.' He started punching me again until a policeman came up . . . We did not sing after this.[78]

Part way through this case Henry Barron entered the court, complaining that he and other witnesses were 'being exposed to the insults and abuses of a mob congregating at the entrance to the Town Hall.' He asked that they be allowed a separate room to wait in. This was agreed.

From accounts from Henry Barron and other witnesses, it appears that the Salvation Army had held a service in the Market Place on the 22nd. When they left, their procession was surrounded by Massagainians making a din with bells, cymbals, rattles, whistles and brass instruments. The trouble started when they reached the corner of Rayleigh Road and Stanley Terrace (Southend Road), where the crowd of Massaganians blocked the road. There was a lot of pushing and shoving and people falling on top of each other.

In his defence, Humphries told the magistrates that he was in front of the Army, who were marching four abreast. He had his back to them:

Edwin Andrews kicked my behind. I turned round. Charles Ford knocked my hat off. I returned the blow. I am quite sure I did nothing to the defendant before this. The Salvation Army persisted in moving along. They could have passed without going through the crowd . . . I carried a brass instrument – I don't know its name – I continually blow it. The Salvation Army have brass instruments as well.[79]

He admitted he struck Andrews four times and Ford once.

After the magistrates had retired 'for a considerable period', Mayor Blatch said:

We have had a long discussion about this case and I am sorry to say that we have not come to anything like a unanimous decision. The minority have, however, to give way to the majority. My brother magistrate, Mr Knight, and myself are of the opinion that a fine of 10s should be sufficient to meet the case; but the decision of the other magistrates is that a fine of £5 be inflicted in each case, or in default one month's imprisonment.

As soon as the decision became known outside the court, 'where an immense body of roughs had assembled, a tumult of a serious character

---

78   Ibid.
79   *Hants and Berks Gazette*, 3 September 1881.

took place, the noise being so great that the business of the court could not for a time be proceeded with.'[80]

The third case was against someone called Goddard for furious driving. On Wednesday 24 August, Goddard drove a horse and cart at an estimated 10 miles an hour through a Salvation Army meeting in Hackwood Road, scattering the worshippers. One unfortunate Salvationist, who did not move fast enough, was knocked down and the wheel of the cart ran over him. Goddard turned the cart round, and when the Salvation Army regrouped in London Street, he whipped up his horse and charged through them again. The magistrates fined him one shilling plus 8s 6d costs, with seven days' in default. (This was not the only instance of riding a horse through the Salvation Army open air meetings. Councillor Tubb was said to have deliberately charged his horse through a Salvation Army procession on at least one occasion.)

The court then adjourned for dinner. When the Mayor left the court, the Massagainians, who were waiting outside, gave him three cheers, which he acknowledged by raising his hat to them, much to the disapproval of the *Gazette*.[81] By contrast, the crowd treated the two Wallises to hisses, insults and threats. At half-past two, when the magistrates returned, the Wallises had to be escorted to the Town Hall by the police and their friends for their own protection.

The last case was a prosecution by Richard Moses against Henry Henwood, William Jones, Joseph Wheatley, Harry Barkham, Richard Humphries, William Digweed, George Bourne, Thomas Cowdery, Charles Hine, Elijah Hockley, Richard Few and Thomas Lloyd for 'violent behaviour' in obstructing the Salvation Army procession on 17 August.

Moses told the court, 'I think they will do me bodily harm. I believe they will get us on the ground and crush us. I go in bodily fear and I believe they will do me and others harm. They may kill me – I can't say.'[82] He asked the court to order the defendants to find sufficient sureties to keep the peace and be of good behaviour.

When the Salvation Army left their barracks on the 17th, marching four abreast along Brook Street, a gang of Massagainians were waiting for them, including the twelve accused. All twelve were playing some rough instrument or other. They elbowed the Salvationists aside to lead the procession and deliberately slow them down. When the Massagainians continued straight on towards Reading Road, the Salvationists turned into Wote Street. The Massagainians turned round and charged up Wote Street after them, pushing the outside members onto the others to regain their

80   Ibid
81   Ibid.
82   Minutes of the Basingstoke Petty Court, 1881–3.

positions at the front, where they continued playing their instruments and shouting and yelling. When the Massagainians went straight on past Potters Lane, the Army turned into the lane and the Massagainians chased after them and barged in front again. The same thing happened when the Massagainians turned right into Church Street and the Salvation Army turned left. The Army were continuously harassed for the rest of their journey along Cross Street, New Street, Winchester Street, Victoria Street, Southern Road, Hackwood Road, London Street, Wote Street to the bottom of Station Hill, and then back along Brook Street. Every now and then, the Massagainians made the procession come to a complete halt. Edward Clayton said the defendants were violent and made several rushes at them. Samuel Frank Johnson complained that Digweed pushed him with his shoulder.[83]

While that case was being heard, a gang of Massaganians had assembled outside the Town Hall. According to George Woodman they 'became uproarious, shouting, hissing, yelling and beating drums, cymbals and rattles'.[84] In fact the noise was so loud that the court had to adjourn to an upper room.

After the closing speeches, the Bench retired for half an hour. On their return, the Mayor said they had thought it advisable to reserve their decision until the following Tuesday.

When they left the court, a hostile crowd, estimated at three or four hundred, surrounded Richard and Arthur Wallis. The crowd followed them through the Market Place and along London Street, jostling them, hissing and jeering, and blowing horns in their faces. *The Gazette* reckoned that, were it not for the protection of the police and their friends, 'they would doubtless have suffered serious injury.' George Woodman wrote that day, 'Town is in a perfect state of riot, everybody trembling with fear.'

That night, police constables were stationed outside Eastlands in London Road (Richard Wallis's home) and Coombehurst in Cliddesden Road (Arthur Wallis's home), to protect their lives and properties. Despite this, a gang of Massagainians gathered by Richard Wallis's gate, playing rough music. Sergeant Waldren arrested Frank Barkham for being drunk and disorderly and crashing his cymbals in Mr Wallis's face. When one of the new magistrates asked if Barkham had any previous convictions, Superintendent Hibberd said that Barkham had never been before them on a charge of drunkenness. Barkham added, 'No gentlemen, I have never been before you before, only with the Salvation Army.'

At ten to eight that night, someone threw a large flint through the plate glass window of Arkas Sapp's shop, narrowly missing a large jar of sulphuric

---

83   Ibid.
84   George Woodman's diary, Willis Museum.

acid and George Woodman, who was standing in the shop at the time. The windows of other Salvation Army supporters were also attacked.[85]

The *Pall Mall Gazette* for 1 September 1881 reported:

> Several men were charged at Basingstoke yesterday with molesting the Salvation Army. One man was fined £10 and costs. On this becoming known a large mob followed two of the magistrates to their homes, pushing them about and threatening their lives. Another magistrate's windows were smashed, and various tradesmen were assaulted.

Richard Wallis wrote to the Home Secretary, enclosing a cutting from the *Gazette* describing the hustling of the magistrates. He said:

> It is a most painful and alarming state of affairs, the object of the roughs and those associated with them is we believe to intimidate some of the magistrates from doing their duty, and my brother and myself seem to be the more particularly the objects of their lawless behaviour, that we feel our persons, and property, may be at any time attacked. The remarks made by the Mayor have, we fear, encouraged rather than discouraged the rioters . . .
>
> I have the honour to subscribe myself for self and four brother magistrates (viz. Messrs A Wallis, T M Kingdon, A Sapp and J B Soper).
>
> Yours most respectfully
> Richard Wallis
>
> P.S. Owing to the extreme hostility of some of the magistrates towards others, we have deemed it prudent to make this communication Private which we trust you will not consider out of order.[86]

The magistrates held a special meeting on 3 September to discuss the disturbances that occurred when the Court was sitting on 30 August. They agreed to ask for six county constables to assist the Borough Police for one month 'to keep order within the precincts of the Court and protect the Justices when necessary.'

John Butler of Bury Farm (Winklebury) later complained to the Council that, owing to the police being fully occupied in protecting the magistrates, his property was not receiving proper protection. While the police were being distracted from their normal duties, some people had broken down one of his hedges in searching for mushrooms!

The following Tuesday (6 September 1881), the twelve defendants returned to the court to receive the magistrates' decision. The Mayor told

85 *Hants and Berks Gazette*, 3 September 1881.
86 TNA PRO HO 45/9607/A2886.

them that the magistrates had decided that they should be bound over to keep the peace and be of good behaviour for a period of three months, themselves in the sum of £5, and one other surety each of £5. They were given two days to find the money and their sureties, or they would be sent to prison for 14 days.

As there was no way that most of those characters would have been capable of keeping the peace for as long as three months, this would have cost the Massagainian fund £120. At ten o'clock on the Thursday morning, ten of the defendants assembled in the Market Place to surrender themselves to their sentence. (One of the twelve had managed to find the money and a surety, and another absconded.[87]) Each of the ten had their summonses framed and hung round their necks and wore hats decorated with coloured ribbons. There was some delay at the Town Hall because Richard Wallis was the only magistrate present who was prepared to sign the committal warrant. Mayor Blatch refused to sign.

Eventually, the ten were marched from the Town Hall to the Police Station, singing all the way. They were locked in the cells until it was time for them to catch their train to Winchester. Shortly after twelve o'clock they were led from the Police Station, handcuffed in pairs, each with a loaf of bread under his free arm. They were headed by an individual carrying what the *Hampshire Chronicle*[88] described as 'The Massagainian Colours' (probably George Tubb's Union Jack). As they marched to the railway station, singing 'Britons never shall be slaves', the streets were lined with cheering crowds waving flags and handkerchiefs. The crowd of well wishers was so great that they had difficulty getting through the doors to the station in order to catch their train to Winchester.[89]

Some 40 or 50 supporters took tickets to Winchester to accompany them to the gates of the gaol. The spectacle of ten men in handcuffs, including 14 year-old Richard Few, with supporters and their police escort, marching merrily from Winchester Station to the county gaol must have astonished the residents of the cathedral city.

On 11 September, George Sclater-Booth, one of the two MPs for North Hampshire, wrote to Adolphus Liddell, the Permanent Secretary at the Home Office, that, together with William Beach, the other member for North Hampshire, he had attended a 'large and influential meeting of the inhabitants of Basingstoke' protesting at the imprisonment of the ten Massagainians. (According to Woodman's diary, the meeting was held at the *Black Boy*.) He said that his view, and that of Mr Beach and the prisoners' solicitor, was that the sentence was 'probably illegal, and

---

87 *Daily News*, 23 September 1881.
88 *Hampshire Chronicle*, 10 September, 1881.
89 *Hants and Berks Gazette*, 10 September 1881.

certainly unjust and impolitic and one which the Secretary of State would probably feel it his duty to remit.' He said, 'it does not appear that anything like an assault was proved or suggested', and 'the feeling of indignation in the town is very deep and participated by many of the most respectable of the inhabitants.'

According to an internal Home Office note from the official who saw Beach and the solicitor the following day, the official pointed out that whether the magistrates had the power to imprison in default of sureties 'was a fine question of law which the S of S could not decide without being advised on the case.' By the time an investigation had taken place, the term of imprisonment would have lapsed. So he had advised them to apply immediately to a Judge in chambers for a Habeas Corpus on the grounds that the men were in illegal custody.

In another hand is written, 'It would never do for the S of S to take one side or the other in this matter. He has told the magistrates what their duty is and how to do it [referring to the advice of 1 April], and beyond that I would not stir a foot.'[90]

It is not known whether William Beach and the solicitor applied to a judge for a Habeas Corpus. If so, nothing happened and the ten prisoners remained in gaol until the end of their sentence.

HAIL THE CONQUERING HEROES COME

Shortly before the prisoners' sentence was due to end, the following notice was circulated around town:

CORN EXCHANGE, BASINGSTOKE
Ten of our Fellow Townsmen having been incarcerated in Winchester Goal [*sic*], in default of finding sureties to keep the peace and be of good behaviour towards Capt. Moses and others of the so-called Salvation Army, it has been resolved to give them a HEARTY RECEPTION on their return, in order to shew them that their Fellow Townsmen do not consider that they are in any way disgraced.
A DINNER
WILL BE HELD
On WEDNESDAY NEXT, the 21st Inst.
AT SEVEN O'CLOCK
which all sympathisers of the party are respectively invited to attend.

Tickets, 1/6 each, to be obtained of the Committee,
who reserve the right to whom the same shall be supplied.

90   TNA PRO HO 45/9607/A2886.

A celebration in the Corn Exchange (Hampshire County Council Museums & Arts Service)

Early in the morning of 21 September 1881, preparations began for the return of the Massagainians. The town was bustling with people erecting flags on the roof of the Corn Exchange and stretching strings of flags and bunting in triumphal arches from one side of Winchester Street to the other. The decorations were in such profusion that the *Gazette* commented that a stranger would have believed that nothing short of a royal entry to the town was about to take place. In the Corn Exchange men were arranging a pyramid of six 36-gallon barrels of XXX beer labelled 'Massagainian Stingo'. Horse-drawn vans continually drew up at the Corn Exchange from various parts of the town to unload vast quantities of meat, fowls, ducks, bottles of wine and other items for a great feast.

Meanwhile in Winchester, news of the ten Massagainian Martyrs had spread around the city and the surrounding countryside. By nine o'clock, when the ten prisoners were released, a crowd estimated at some four or five hundred were waiting outside the prison gates to welcome them to freedom. Headed by a Union Jack, the crowd escorted them to the *Plume of Feathers*, near the Westgate, where a breakfast was provided for them. Later, after what was described as 'a capital dinner', presided over by Edward and Valentine Adams, they climbed into a grand coach drawn by four horses driven by John Tubb, George Tubb's brother, the owner of the Winchester livery stables. They set off for Basingstoke at half-past two, to the sound of a large blast on the coaching horn.

Back in Basingstoke, by four o'clock an enormous crowd had gathered to welcome the Massagainians home. A gaggle of young women waited on the Town Hall balcony watching the outriders 'dressed in gay scarlet' and a band of musicians brought in from Reading heading off down Winchester Street to meet the returning Massagainians. At half-past five a lad on a penny-farthing rode into town shouting, 'They're just behind!' Soon the sound of the band playing 'Hail The Conquering Heroes Come' reached the ears of the waiting crowd. A great cheer sprang up as the procession came into sight – a cart driven by William White the horse-breaker containing the band, followed by the outriders and the coach with the Massagainians on board. As they passed the Town Hall, the women on the balcony waved their handkerchiefs like maidens at a medieval tournament. The coach delivered the returning prisoners to the Corn Exchange, where they were hoisted on the shoulders of their supporters and carried inside.

Unhappily, William White missed his dinner. Shortly after he delivered the band, he was arrested on a charge of receiving stolen beans and oats. When his case came to Court, he was sentenced to two months' hard labour.

At seven o'clock the Corn Exchange was packed to bursting point. 521 people sat down to enjoy the feast. Allowing for supporters who had volunteered to act as waiters, the *Hampshire Chronicle* estimated there were 600 people present. Charles Ayliffe of May Place chaired the proceedings, supported by Alfred White, the auctioneer, as his vice-chair. Among those present were the three Adams brothers, Councillor Tubb and his brother John, Councillor John Lodwidge, Simon Westcott the Borough Surveyor, William Raynbird the estate manager at Hackwood Park, Albert Portsmouth the Wote Street ironmonger, May and Catherine Powell (later, Mrs Edward Adams), aged 23 and 21 respectively, and Miss Gregory of Winchester Street (who were probably among the young ladies who graced the Town Hall balcony), and a number of prominent farmers and millers from the outlying villages.

When the last course was finished ('Massagainian Puddings all on fire'), and the tables cleared, the Chairman proposed a toast for the Queen and the Royal Family. Charles Hine, one of the returning Massagainians, then stood up and sang 'There's Bound To Be A Row' to rapturous applause. The Chairman then proposed a toast to the Army, Navy and the Reserve Forces. Sergeant Hitchcock of the Reserves responded by singing 'Sweet Violets'. The next toast was 'The ladies and the donors of subscriptions', given by George Brooks of Manor Farm, Monk Sherborne. This was followed by Thomas Powers, the Winchester Road saddler, singing 'When We Were Boys Together', and William Easton, Alderman Allen's assistant, singing 'We Don't Want To Fight, But By Jingo If We Do'. John Butler of Bury Farm proposed a toast to the Chairman, who in turn proposed a toast to the health and prosperity of the men just liberated from gaol, acknowledging the attempts of the two North Hampshire MPs and the Vicar of Basingstoke to persuade the Home Secretary to reverse the magistrates' decision, and stating that the fund would pay the men's wages lost during their imprisonment. According to George Woodman, each man was presented with a silver watch.

By this time in the proceedings, copious amounts of Massagainian Stingo and the other booze on offer had been drunk and all was merry. It was time to sing 'The Massagainian Song', the lyrics of which had been printed on handbills especially for the occasion:

When Barren gets up in his rostrum,
 The brewers he sends to old Nick,
'Drink coffee or tea' is the nostrum,
 He tries down our throttles to stick;
But for Barren and such like asses,
 We care not a fig what they say;
And still go on filling our glasses,
 With stingo from Adams or May!
Then a fig for such fools and their lingo,
 We care not a jot what they say,
 So John Bull, fill right full,
With Barley-corn from Adams, Barrett or May.

Old Barren with arguments shallow
 May tell us there's death in the glass,
His coffee and tea let him swallow,
 I much prefer Allsopp or Bass;
Let Barren go preach against drinking,
 I heed not a word he may say,
No liquor yet beat to my thinking,
 The stingo of Adams or May,
Then a fig for such fools and their lingo,
 We care not a jot what they say,
 So John Bull, fill right full,
With Barley-corn from Adams, Barrett or May.

At Eastrop you'll find the great Richard,
 Who strives to be king in this place,
His eyes on the pavement are fixed hard,
 He can't look you straight in the face;
Some mischief he's ever contriving,
 And were we by him to be led,
The Curfew he'd vote for reviving,
 And send us like schoolboys to bed,
Then a fig for such fools and their lingo,

We care not a jot what they say,
So John Bull, fill right full,
With Barley-corn from Adams, Barrett or May.

'Tis whispered when Richard was younger
He played some queer pranks in his time,
But now, he's a chicken no longer,
He looks on a laugh as a crime;
Oh! Richard you must be a noddy,
More charity sure you'd display,
If you'd now and then warm your old body,
With stingo from Adams or May,
Then a fig for such fools and their lingo,
We care not a jot what they say,
So John Bull, fill right full,
With Barley-corn from Adams, Barrett or May.

Then comrades make ready your glasses,
And charge them right up to the brim,
If Barren and Richard be asses,
We need not take pattern by 'thim';
May the flag that is now waving o'er us,
The 'red, white, and blue' long display,
And may we oft toast it in chorus,
With stingo from Adams or May,
Then a fig for such fools and their lingo,
We care not a jot what they say,
So John Bull, fill right full,
With Barley-corn from Adams, Barrett or May.
(I wish I knew the tune.)

After the song was over, the Chairman proposed a toast to the health
of the Committee of the Management, during which he thanked Simon
Westcott for making the arrangements for the dinner. William Pearson, a
solicitor's clerk, sang 'The Lifeboat'. The next toast was 'The health of the
Vice-Chairman'. William Leavey, the landlord of the *Railway Arms* then
entertained the hall by singing that he was 'The Chap For A Spree'. The
final toast was 'The health of the visitors', to which John Tubb responded
that if ever the Salvation Army came to Winchester, 'they would have it
much worse than they had it in Basingstoke.'

At 10.30, after three and a half hours of solid drinking, the six hundred
tumbled out of the Corn Exchange. Somehow a window got broken; it is
not clear whether this was high spirits or an accident. The evening had

The Borough Police Station in New Street
(Hampshire County Council Museums & Arts Service)

been a good natured, if noisy occasion, and everyone might have gone home with very little trouble if Sergeant Waldren had not decided to hit a man in the mouth, the reason for which is unclear. This was the spark that set off a minor riot. Sergeant Waldren was pushed and buffeted around the Market Place. Someone stole his helmet, and some of the lads used it as a football, kicking it around the street.[91] Someone else threw a stone through one of the windows of the Town Hall. Some of the crowd rightly or wrongly got into their heads that Sergeant Waldren had partaken too freely of the Massagainian Stingo. They pushed him towards the Police Station, shouting, 'Lock him away, he's drunk' – a classic case of the pot calling the kettle black.

Superintendent Hibberd came out and rescued his sergeant and got him safely inside the Police Station. He then stood on the station steps, exhorting the crowd to go home peaceably. The crowd responded by smashing the Police Station windows. The Superintendent then had the

---

91   Manuscript paper, *The Salvation Army Riots*, written by Arthur Hailstone in 1945 for the London Street Congregational Church.

presence of mind to tell them that if they would at once go home like good
fellows, he would lead the way. Surprisingly that worked. There was no real
animosity towards the Borough Police (unlike the way they felt about the
County Police), and the crowd dispersed to their homes at the end of an
eventful day.[92]

Once again news from Basingstoke made the national press. Some
mischievous stringer had sent a telegram to the Central News Agency
that there had been a tremendous riot, the mob having possession of the
town for several hours, and that the police had been powerless. There were
reports in the *Daily Telegraph*, the *Standard*, *Daily Chronicle* and the *Daily
News*. The *Daily News* began its story:

> On Wednesday night the town of Basingstoke was the scene of a
> disgraceful riot. Windows were broken, the police assaulted, and a
> disorderly mob paraded the streets without let or hindrance.

News of the dinner was even reported in an Irish newspaper.[93]

The *Winchester Observer* criticised the Town Council for letting the
Corn Exchange for the Massagainian Banquet:

> The novel experiment which Basingstoke is making in the mode
> of self-government will be watched with some interest. The rough
> has been elevated into the place of the policeman . . . the town has
> sympathised with him on being committed to prison for asserting
> mob law, and feted him as a martyr and a hero when he came out
> . . . Civilisation has doubtless restraints which the free spirits of
> Basingstoke would like to see removed.

A letter to the *Hants and Berks Gazette* on 1 October 1881 somewhat
overstated the case when it said that the dinner for the 'Massagainian
Martyrs' had 'made the name of Basingstoke a disgrace throughout the
civilised world'.

On the Saturday night, the ten released prisoners met in the bar of the
Shades (later the *Victoria Inn*), where Simon Westcott, who doubled in the
role of Borough Surveyor and Treasurer of the Massagainian Fund, doled
out £1 each to the married men and 10 shillings to the single men.

---

92   Most of this detail comes from the *Hants and Berks Gazette* and the
Hampshire Chronicle for 24 September 1881.
93   *Freeman's Journal* (Dublin), 24 September, 1881.

THE ELECTION RIOT

The municipal election was held on 1 November 1881. This was the first time since the March riots and the August petitions that the divisions in the town could be translated into votes. In the weeks leading up to the election, it was clear that it was going to be a very close contest, as the town was polarised as never before. George Woodman summed up the mood of the town when he reported in his diary:

> Municipal Election. A fiercely contested one, the first time it had been fought politically, Tory against Liberals, Churchmen against dissenters, temperance against drink, Massagainians against the Salvation Army.

John Burgess Soper had already anticipated trouble. At the magistrates' meeting on 11 October, he 'gave information on oath' that he apprehended a riot and disturbance on the first of November. He asked the magistrates to agree to apply to Captain Forest for nine County Police to be sworn as special constables for that day.

Before nine o'clock on the morning of the election, carriages, vans and vehicles of every description, blazoned with their candidates' names, were tearing about in all directions to bring their voters to the polling room. During the day groups of lads alternated between their pubs and the Liberals' headquarters at the teetotal Old Angel Café, where they stood outside, ringing bells and making 'blasphemous comments'.[94] When polling ended at four o'clock, the streets began to empty while the count took place inside the Town Hall.

From six o'clock knots of people began to reappear in the Market Place, speculating about the result, most expecting that, of the eight candidates fighting for four seats, the two parties would win two seats each. By seven o'clock a large crowd had gathered outside the Town Hall, waiting for the results to be announced. Among them was a group of about 200 Massagainians, many of whom had been drinking all day. They were shouting insults at the committee members going in and out of the Old Angel Café. Spencer Doman lobbed a stone, smashing one of the large plate glass windows of the Café. It was Spencer's bad luck that PC Simpson and

94 *Hants and Berks Gazette*, 5 November 1881.

PC George Paice were standing only a couple of yards behind him, and caught him red handed.

Shortly afterwards, the results of the poll were announced. The number of votes each candidate received was as follows: Temple, 450; Lodwidge, 447; Follett, 441; Webb, 426; Burberry, 415; Smith, 412; Schofield, 391; Jackson, 379. The first four, all Conservatives, were declared the duly elected members for the next three years. As George Woodman recorded, 'The Massagainian Party gained the day; dissenters defeated.'

As soon as the result was declared, the crowd of jubilant Massagainians went on the rampage. In the words of the *Reading Mercury* on 5 November, 'a series of dastardly outrages was at once entered upon'. They paraded along London Street to Eastlands, where Richard Wallis lay dangerously ill. (Richard Wallis died on 28 November 1881. Although he was a Quaker, his coffin was carried by six members of the Salvation Army.)

Finding no fun at Eastlands, the Massagainians turned back and went along London Street, stopping outside the homes of Alderman Allen and the newly re-elected Councillor Webb to give three cheers. They then hurried off to Essex Road to smash Henry Barron's windows. Mr and Mrs Barron were out. Annie Simpson, their servant, was alone in the house with the Barrons' young children. Luckily, she had the presence of mind to carry the children into the back bedroom. As she was doing so, a stone crashed through the front bedroom window, hitting her on the arm.

The Massagainians then surged down Brook Street to the Salvation Army factory. About 200 people were inside listening to a talk from Major Moore, who had just returned from America. As soon as they heard the Massagainians coming, they barricaded the door. The Massagainians tried to break it down. They smashed the gas lamps and the windows, showering the congregation with glass. Some even tried to break in through the roof.

Their next stop was the Brewery House, where they stood outside, giving three hearty cheers for the Mayor. From there they turned the corner into Chapel Street, where George Greenaway, 'The Hallelujah Auctioneer' – a Salvation Army soldier – had his shop. Using building materials from a house being repaired just opposite, they smashed every window at the front of the house, and struck a heavy blow at the front door, which knocked the catch of the door fastening clean out. The shutters of the shop were closed; otherwise the damage would have been far worse. During the bombardment, George Greenaway's wife and aged father felt obliged to flee out of the back door for safety.

The next stop was Hillside, John Burgess Soper's house in Vyne Road.

*Hillside, commonly known as 'Soper's Castle', after the election riot, 1 November 1881.
(Hampshire County Council Museums & Arts Service)*

THE SIEGE OF SOPER'S CASTLE

Amy Westbrook, John Burgess Soper's maid, was in the Market Place at
seven o'clock that evening to hear the results of the election. As she passed
a crowd of people she heard one of them say, 'We'll go up to bloody old
Soper's and burn the bloody house down.'

She ran all the way to Hillside (known as Soper's Castle because of its
crenellated walls) to warn the household. Sarah, Soper's daughter, and
Soper's invalid sister were the only people in the house. Amy and Sarah
reckoned that, as there was no woodwork on the exterior of the house, if the
mob wanted to burn the house down, they would have to get inside. So they
locked the doors and turned the gas out. In a race against time they did their
best to move the heavy Victorian furniture to barricade the doors. When
the Massagainians arrived, they started throwing rocks at the windows in
the front of the house. The two frightened women sheltered in the back
kitchen, listening to the sounds of breaking glass and the Massagainians
trying to break down the front door. When the Massagainians moved round
and started throwing stones through the back windows, Amy and Sarah
retreated to the back bedroom to where the bedridden old lady lay. (The old
lady died on 12 November. In a letter to the Home Secretary, Soper said he
believed the shock hastened her death. According to George Woodman her
last words were, 'They are coming; they are coming.')

Henry Smith's Musical Instrument Warehouse after the election riots of 1 November 1881.
(Robert Brown)

The Massagainians smashed all twelve windows, containing 126 feet of plate glass, and broke the blinds. Three times they tried to enter the house, but each time the locks and the barricades held. They tried to set fire to the house, but the fires did not take hold. Later that night, when Soper arrived home, he found 53 large stones in various rooms, including one on his bed weighing over 2lbs, and one on the mantelpiece that had smashed some of his ornaments. He estimated the mob had caused £29 10s worth of damage to his house[95] – at least £1,800 in today's money (2010).

In a letter to the Home Secretary, Soper said he was a marked man because he was the only member of the corporation that objected to the use of the Corn Exchange for the Massagainian Banquet and because he called for the County Police to help keep the peace on election day. He said, 'I now go about in personal bodily fear. In fact my family will not allow me out after dark.'[96]

Having delivered a parting volley of stones at Soper's Castle, the Massagainians went back into town. Down Station Hill they smashed the plate glass window of Councillor Henry Smith's musical instrument warehouse, making holes large enough for a man to crawl through. Then on to Bunnian Place, where Councillor Schofield lived. They smashed his windows with sticks and stones, breaking a window frame in the process. As they passed Gerrish, Ames and Simpkins' clothing factory they smashed

---

95   Minutes of the Basingstoke Petty Court, 1881–3 and TNA PRO HO 45/9607/A2886.

96   TNA PRO HO 45/9607/A2886.

two or three panes of glass, likewise at Wallis's foundry where five or six panes were broken.

They broke several panes in the window of the Wesleyan Chapel, and on their way up Church Street they broke six or seven panes of glass at James Felgate's Gospel Book Depot and one of Sterry Wallis's windows. Someone threw a large stone through the front window of the *Gazette* Office, damaging the wire blinds. And just as PC Early, a County policeman, came along, one stone crashed through the bedroom window, and then another smashed the glass of the front door. PC Early saw the man who threw the last two stones and he pinned him against the wall. PC Early was surrounded by people shouting, 'Down with the bloody County Police' and 'Kill the Buggers'. Someone hit him on the side of the head with a stone. Another stone hit him in the mouth, cutting his upper lip, but he still did not relinquish his grip on the prisoner, until Sergeant Waldren came along and recognised the culprit as William Varndell, a shoemaker from Milward's factory. Sergeant Waldren later said that he recognised Charles Hine and Albert Lansley among the crowd in Church Street.[97]

The Massagainians' last port of call was Arkas Sapp's shop at the top of town. They banged their sticks against the iron shutters protecting the shop. According to George Woodman, 'The row they made with their big sticks to us inside was terrible.'

George Woodman's diary for the following day read, 'Great commotion about last night's disgraceful conduct. People going round to see what damage was done.'

Someone who styled himself 'Observer' had a wonderfully melodramatic letter published in the *Hants and Berks Gazette* for 12 November 1881:

> November 1st was a red letter day for shameful rowdyism in the already notorious town of Basingstoke . . . During the earlier part of the day matters went on as orderly as may reasonably be expected. But later on it became evident that the lamb-like hirelings of the respectable rowdies meant business, having been primed liberally for the occasion. Persons who had the misfortune to be suspected of holding opinions diverse from King Mob were openly insulted, and even ladies were saluted with language too vile and filthy to repeat. The success which attended the party of disorder, was as great a surprise to them as to their opponents, but as a shindy had been planned in case of defeat, it was too much for their paid and devoted adherents to forego the luxury. So after sundry jostling and shovings in and about the Market-place, they openly declared their mission of mischief; which bordered dangerously near upon murder.

97   *Hants and Berks Gazette*, 5 November 1881 and Minutes of the Basingstoke Petty Court, 1881–3.

One or two of these harmless sucklings were caught in the – to them – pleasing act of throwing stones at glass, testing its powers of resistance. Yet nothing daunted, they pursued to the end and completed the task allotted, and such a completion as would have gratified the most savage and ferocious barbarian. Private houses and places of worship, the residence of a minister of religion, and also of four councillors, and that of a justice of the peace, were objects of this fiendish savagery. Truly that was a night of horror, never to be forgotten. When the light of the morning revealed the result of this paid for pastime, it was a scene to be remembered. It was as if the devoted houses had stood in the line of battle and had been battered by shot and shell. Large stones, 4 or 5 lbs each lay about inside and out by scores. Nearly whole bricks were hurled, smashing glass and window frames to the imminent danger to the lives of the inmates. One poor old bedridden lady, unable to move hand or foot, was frightened all but to death by the crashing of stones through the thick plate glass into her bedroom. Scarcely a whole pane of glass was left in the house, up stairs or down – a complete wreck – splendid glass worth £6 or £8 each scattered in atoms inside and out of the houses. Many persons went next morning to look at the ruins; amongst the rest, the instigators to the riot looking as innocent as possible, and expressing their horror, and repudiating all connection and participation in it! . . . Does one of these cowardly scoundrels recognise his handy-work, for which he offered 6d each to his hire-lings? . . . Much more might, and perhaps will, be said. The day of retribution draweth nigh. The righteous can afford to suffer and wait.

There was a general complaint that the police were ineffective. After the election results were announced, the police were taken to the Town Hall to eat their supper. While they were inside, enjoying their refreshments, the Massagainians were out on the rampage. When the police heard that the Massagainians were attacking the Salvation Army barracks, they headed down to Brook Street. But by the time they got there, the Massagainians had moved on. The police did not come into contact with the Massagainians until they met in Church Street, by which time the Massagainians had completed their night of destruction.

There was also criticism that Superintendent Hibberd had been sent away to Reading to inquire about a stolen horse. John Burgess Soper said that the police had been 'decoyed away by refreshments', this, and the fact that 'the Superintendent was actually, and indiscreetly sent away by the Mayor to Reading . . . are looked upon with some considerable suspicion.'[98]

---

98   TNA PRO HO 45/9607/A2886.

As a result of the election riot, Basingstoke enjoyed another fifteen minutes of fame in the national and provincial press, including the *Western Mail* and the *Birmingham Daily Post*. *Reynolds' Newspaper* made matters seem worse than they actually were when it reported that 'a mob numbering about 200 assembled, went through the town, and deliberately smashed a number of widows [*sic*].' [99]

At the beginning of November, Captain Moses left Basingstoke to take over the Darlington corps of the Salvation Army from Captain William Fenny. In a straight swap, Captain Fenny took charge in Basingstoke. At about the same time, William Blatch's tenure as Mayor was over, but as ex-Mayor, he remained on the magistrate's bench. John Lodwidge, the ironmonger, was elected the new Mayor.

NOTE: The details in this chapter come from a variety of sources, mainly the Hants and Berks Gazette *and the Minutes of the Basingstoke Petty Court, 1881–3.*

99   *Reynolds' Newspaper*, 6 November 1881.

THE CHARGE OF THE BASINGSTOKE

BEER BRIGADE

A serious disturbance, in connection with the Salvation Army procession, occurred in Basingstoke yesterday. The members of the Army of both sexes and known supporters were seriously beaten and rolled in a muddy stream. The townspeople who dared remonstrate were treated in like manner. No arrests were made among the assailants, but the 'Captain' and another person with the Army were given into custody by Mr Councillor Knight, J.P. Two other magistrates were present, and, being known as having tried to afford protection for the Army, were threatened and hooted, and had to take refuge in the residence of another magistrate near the scene of the riot. The 'Captain' of the Army was afterwards released.

Pall Mall Gazette, 6 March 1882

The Salvation Army abandoned its open air meetings. But by February 1882 the numbers attending its indoor services had fallen. This may have been partly due to the group of youths who used to hang around outside the factory at service time, shouting insults. It was said that one lad used to indecently expose himself to the congregation as they entered the factory door. So the Salvation Army London Headquarters ordered Captain Fenny to get back out onto the streets.

Having wind of this and taking the mood of the town, Superintendent Hibberd told the magistrates that he expected there would be a riot if the Salvation Army held the procession they planned for Sunday 19 February. On 14 February, the magistrates, chaired by Mayor Lodwidge, hastily convened a special meeting, at which they unanimously resolved to issue an order that:

> . . . serious breaches of the Peace are anticipated by reason of certain persons designating themselves members of the Salvation Army parading the streets in Public Procession and the interference therewith of persons opposed to such procession:-
> NOTICE IS HEREBY GIVEN, – That no such Procession will in future be permitted within the said Town, and the leaders of the Procession and all other persons who intend to take part in it are hereby required and directed to abstain from joining in it;
> AND NOTICE IS HEREBY GIVEN, – That all persons are

J. W. Lodwidge (Hampshire County Council Museums & Arts Service)

required to abstain from assembling for the purpose of interference
with such Procession, and from loitering or causing a crowd to
collect with that object;

AND NOTICE IS HEREBY FURTHER GIVEN, – That the
Police . . . have received strict orders to prevent and disperse such
Procession, assemblage, or loitering of persons, and to take all
necessary steps for that purpose, and otherwise to preserve the peace
and good order of the Town.

On the 19th at 10 a.m. the Salvation Army held a prayer meeting outside
Captain Fenny's house in Newtown (now Brookvale). They were silently
observed by a group of Massagainians. Just as the Salvationists were rising
from their knees, Superintendent Hibberd arrived and ordered them to
disperse. The Salvationists refused to move. So the Massagainians decided
to do the police's job for them by pushing Captain Fenny in the direction
of the factory.

The Salvation Army attempted to form a procession, but were
prevented by the Massagainians infiltrating their ranks and isolating the
soldiers from each other. After much pushing and shoving, during which
Captain Fenny was knocked to the ground twice and had his hat stolen, the
Salvationists reached the safety of their factory, but not before the Captain
announced that he would be holding a meeting in Flaxfield at two o'clock
that afternoon.

That lunchtime, news of the intended meeting spread round the pubs.

Before two o'clock, some five or six hundred had gathered in Flaxfield Road, waiting for the fun to start. In the words of the *Hants and Berks Gazette*,:

> Drink certainly had created some very fiendish intentions in the minds of those who had arrived to break up the procession.[100]

At two o'clock the Salvation Army marched out again and held a meeting outside the *Hare and Hounds*. In the words of George Woodman:

> SA came out in opposition to the proclamation and got most brutally ill-treated. I saw them, many without hats and many covered in mud.

From the testimony of Superintendent Hibberd in the Magistrates' Court, the procession stopped outside the *Hare and Hounds*, the Salvationists placed handkerchiefs on the road and got on their knees, presumably to pray for the drinkers inside. Hibberd told Fenny:

> 'You must all move on, you are breaking the law, stopping up the road.'
> Fenny replied, 'Then lock me up, I shall not move on.'
> 'It is not a lock up case, but I ask you all to move on and disperse and not block the road.'

The Army stayed on its knees. In the confusion of pushing and shoving, Frank Barkham fell down on top of Fenny, and four or five other persons fell down together in a heap. Hibberd shouted, 'Don't kill the man!' He managed to pull them apart and push them away from each other. He pulled Fenny up and, calling on Constable Mears, told Fenny, 'The constable and I will take you back safe to the Factory.' Fenny answered, 'I shall not be taken there. I shall not go.' Edward Clayton and Francis and Herbert Gear also refused to move when asked. Two of his friends took Frank Barkham away to his home for his own good. But he soon returned.[101]

As the Salvationists refused to leave, and the excited crowd were milling around, the police were powerless to enforce the magistrates' proclamation. In the confusion a group of Massagainians tried to push Captain Fenny over the hedge into the stream that used to flow past the bottom of Flaxfield Road. That failed. But then the milling crowd crushed him against the houses opposite, and he was badly hurt. His supporters rescued him and took him to a nearby house to recover.

Francis Gear said he tried to assist Captain Fenny, 'but was attacked myself and had difficulty keeping my legs.' He saw 'ten or twelve roughs' beating his son, Herbert, with their fists and sticks. Herbert Gear said he shouted out to PC Trodd to help him, but the policeman simply said, 'No

---

100   *Hants and Berks Gazette*, 25 February 1882.
101   Minutes of the Basingstoke Petty Court, 1881–3.

striking here.' 'They ran after me and got me in a gutter, in which position they got on top of me. They beat me about the head until I was rescued by friends.' The Massagainians tried to put Francis Gear in the water, 'and would have succeeded had it not been for the hedge which divided the road from the stream.'[102]

Without their Captain, the Salvationists fled towards the factory down Essex Road. The Massagainians managed to grab hold of one or two of the soldiers and attempted to duck them in the stream that ran across the meadows in front of Bath Terrace, and is now culverted under Victory Roundabout.

Following the events of the 19th, seven people were summonsed for 'loitering on the thoroughfare and refusing to move on when requested', but only two were Massagainians – Frank and Harry Barkham. The rest were Salvation Army members – Captain Fenny, Daniel Goodall, Edward Clayton and Francis and Herbert Gear.

The lawyers acting for both sets of defendants successfully pleaded that, although copies of the notice of the Order of the 14th were displayed all over the town, a copy was not displayed in the office of the Clerk to the Local Government Board, contrary to the 129th section of the Act of 11 and 12 Vic., c.63. On that technicality, the magistrates had no alternative than to acquit all seven defendants.[103]

The events of the 19th inspired the *Gazette* to print this parody of Tennyson:

THE CHARGE OF THE BASINGSTOKE BEER BRIGADE

[FEBRUARY 19th 1882]

Glory to Basingstoke!
Once more the Army's broke
By the Two Hundred.
Forward the Beer Brigade,
Charge the saints, someone said,
Noble Two Hundred.

Not like the Berkshire brave
Turned they at bay to save
Regiments in flight.
No dread of deadly strife,
No fear of Afghan knife,

102   TNA PRO HO 45/9607/A2886.
103   *Hants and Berks Gazette*, 4 March 1882 and Minutes of the Basingstoke Petty Court, 1881–3.

All were too sure of life,
All that Two Hundred.

Foes theirs that would not arm,
Foes theirs that could not harm,
Foes that would always charm
Such a Two Hundred.
Foes that would strike no blow,
Yea, no resistance show
At them you safely go,
Gallant Two Hundred.

Charge, then, and don't turn tail,
Don't let your courage fail,
Brave be with May's Pale Ale
Noble Two Hundred.
On, then, for finest fun,
On, then, to glory run,
Do not such foemen shun,
Gallant Two Hundred.

Pelt, throw, and aim your blow,
At the helpless, harmless foe,
Let them no mercy know,
Glorious Two Hundred.
Wound the women, maim the men,
Care not for children then,
So they pray not here again
Trusty Two Hundred.

What though the Mayor stand here,
He will never interfere,
On then you men of beer,
Beery Two Hundred.
How dare they strive to save
Yeomen from the drink they crave!
On, then, at once ye brave
Gallant Two Hundred.

Forward the Beer Brigade!
Was there a man dismayed?
Not though the drinker knew
Someone had thundered.

Their's not to question why,
Their's but to do, not die,
Down the street for the saints
Roll the Two Hundred.

Friends to the right of them,
Friends to the left of them,
Friends all around them,
Encouragement thundered!
On they go one and all,
Urged by their leader's call,
On for the Mission Hall,
Gallant Two Hundred.

On then they madly rush
Eager their weak foe to crush,
Charging an Army.
While all the world wondered;
Fighting the praying folk
Right through the line they broke,
Captain and private
Reeled from their reckless stroke
Shattered and sundered,
Then they came back – yea all,
All that Two Hundred.

When can their glory fade?
Oh the wild charge they made
All the world wondered,
Honour the charge they made,
Honour the Beer Brigade,
Noble Two Hundred.

Thus gloried Basingstoke,
Such were the words it spoke.
Glory to Basingstoke!

Shame rather Basingstoke,
That it should be willing
To let the mob rule –
At least that's what Brown says,
And he mostly right is,
And never a fool.

For if they are willing
To hinder such killing,
The Mayor, beaks and bobbies,
And men of the law,
Aye, citizens too, of every grade,

Then why do they seem sadly afraid
To tackle with vigour the Beery Brigade.
That coward, unmanly Brigade.
Glory's the word Brown spoke?
Shame only Basingstoke! [104]

(Presumably 'Brown' was George Brown of the *Royal Exchange*.)
    On 23 February 1882 Captain Fenny wrote to Thomas Maton Kingdon:

> My Dear Sir,
> Kindly permit me to say that the Salvation Army will meet in the
> Market Place on Sunday morning at 10 o'clock.
>   God bless you
>   Yours Humbly
>   Captain Fenny.

The magistrates replied drawing Captain Fenny's attention to the Order
and told him that such a meeting would be unlawful and steps would be
taken to prevent or disperse the meeting. Superintendent Hibberd told the
magistrates that he feared there would be a serious disturbance and he did
not have enough men to keep the peace. The magistrates asked for 20 County
Police to be sworn in as special constables to assist the Borough Police.[105]
    At nine o'clock on the Sunday morning the 20 County policemen, who
had been fetched over from Winchester the night before, were sworn in
as special constables in the Town Hall. By five to ten a crowd estimated
at between five or six hundred had gathered in the vicinity of the Market
Place, waiting to see if the Salvation Army would appear. They were
surprised to see the 20 County policemen troop out of the Town Hall.
Then, just as the clock struck ten, the Salvation Army came into view,
marching up Church Street. The Army and its supporters reached the
Market Place unmolested. But as Captain Fenny announced the singing of
a hymn, the police ordered the Army to disperse, followed by an order that
no service would be permitted. On which the crowd gave a great cheer,
described by the *Gazette* as 'a roar of victory and menace combined.'
    The Army tried to march along London Street, but their path was
blocked. Instead, they were forced down Church Street, closely followed

---

104   *Hants and Berks Gazette*, 4 March 1882.
105   Minutes of the Basingstoke Petty Court, 1881–3.

by the police and 'an excited mob'. After a great deal of pushing and shoving, the Massagainians managed to knock the Captain over. A group of policemen barged through the crowd to set him back on his feet. In the crush caused by this abrupt halt, the press of people caused one of the shop windows to smash. Eventually, the factory was reached without any serious incident and the crowd quietly dispersed.

During the next few hours the town was alive with speculation about what was likely to happen that afternoon when the pubs would be open, drink would have been taken, and the morning's crowd would have been augmented by those who had spent the morning sleeping off the night before and by lads from the villages.

By two o'clock a large crowd had assembled in the Market Place waiting for the trouble to start. When the Salvation Army came in sight as they came up Church Street, a large portion of the crowd rushed down the hill towards them, hotly pursued by a body of police. Before too many blows had been struck the police managed to separate the opposing parties and forced the crowd back up Church Street. Once the police and the Salvation Army and its supporters had reached the Market Place, some 1,500 people were milling around, but the anger of the crowd was directed more at the County Police than at the Salvationists.

Someone punched PC Trusler in the face, at the same time shouting, 'Let the bastards have it, coppers and all.' PC Trusler seized him, and with assistance from other officers, rushed him into the Town Hall. A group of Massagainians tried to rescue him, but in vain. A threatening crowd began angrily shouting at the entrance to the Town Hall. A nervous Mayor Lodwidge read the Riot Act to try to disperse the crowd, but was met with contemptuous laughter.

While the crowd was thus distracted, the Salvation Army managed to get down Church Street before their retreat was discovered. They were soon spotted. Some men and boys ran after them, and they, in turn, were chased by a group of policemen. In a scene worthy of the Keystone Cops, the remaining police, perhaps unfamiliar with the layout of the town, formed a line across the top of Church Street to prevent anyone else pursuing the retreating Salvationists. Instead, the crowd headed for the bottom end of Church Street by racing down Wote Street and along Potters Lane to join the fun. Realising that their thin blue line was not meeting its intended purpose, the policemen ran down Church Street to join their colleagues. The police managed to drive the Massgainians away from the Salvation Army. They escorted the Army back to the factory with no bones broken.

The following day, Charles Purdue, a farm labourer living at the *Self Defence* public house, appeared before the magistrates, charged with assaulting PC Trusler. After the evidence was heard, the magistrates moved to an adjoining room to consider their verdict. On their return, the Mayor announced, 'Charles Purdue, your case has been very carefully considered, and the magistrates feel they must put a stop to these disgraceful proceedings. You must pay a fine of £2 including costs, or go to prison for one month with hard labour.' He was given until the evening to find the money. but later that day, George Brown of the Royal Exchange public house, paid his fine.[106]

On 2 March, Captain Fenny sent another letter to T. M. Kingdon, announcing his intention to hold meetings in the Market Place the following Sunday at ten and two o'clock. Superintendent Hibberd told the magistrates that he, Sergeant Waldren, and their five constables were sufficient to keep the peace the following Sunday.[107] Bringing in the County Police the last weekend had cost the borough ratepayers some £20.

On the morning of Sunday 5 March the Salvation Army and its followers marched out from the factory. When they arrived at the Market Square, the police and a gang of Massagainians were waiting for them. When Captain Fenny announced a hymn, the police broke up the meeting by pushing the Salvationists in the direction of Church Street, while the crowd encouraged the police with cries of, 'Give it to 'em, Mark.' Once or twice the Superintendent turned to the crowd behind him saying, 'You chaps leave off pushing, we'll do the work.' However, some of the Massagainians managed to knock the Captain down and rolled him in the mud, but he was rescued before 'they would assuredly have trampled him to death'. The Constables made a ring around the Army and escorted them safely to the factory without any further harm.

According to William Fenny:

> The Superintendent of Police and Police Constable Mears at
> once came to me and violently severed me from my wife, the mob
> then turned upon us, and violently assaulted us by punching, &c.
> I received violent blows from various members of the mob, and
> therefore called on the Superintendent of Police for help, to which
> he replied, 'You have no right to come out; you are the breakers of
> the law.'[108]

George Woodman, an eye-witness to the morning's events, was shocked to see that some of the most enthusiastic attackers were people he had hitherto regarded as respectable, including Seth Lawes, the local plumber.

When the Army attempted another procession in the afternoon, a crowd, estimated at about 2,000, were waiting for them in the Market Place – a mixture of supporters, sightseers who had turned up in the hope of

106 *Hants and Berks Gazette*, 4 March 1882.
107 Minutes of the Basingstoke Petty Court,1881–3.
108 TNA PRO HO 45/9607/A2886.

enjoying watching another fight, and Massaganians – 'amongst them were most of the characters who were conspicuous as the leaders of the riots in March, and a degraded villainous lot they looked.'[109] When the Salvation Army reached the Market Place they were greeted by catcalls and booing. The Salvation Army linked arms and began singing hymns. Captain Fenny claimed Superintendent Hibberd assaulted him and his wife when he tried to part them:

> The Superintendent of Police again assaulted me by roughly pushing me about; the roughs then followed his example and pushed me with great violence against the wall, knocked me down, and kicked me, causing blood to flow from me freely.[110]

PC Hurst said that, during his attempts to stop the Salvation Army from linking arms, Mrs Fenny struck him in the mouth. When the police broke up the procession, the Salvationists were scattered amongst the crowd so the Massaganians could not attack them in a body. But 'whenever one or two of them were seen, the roughs made a rush at them in a most infuriated and dastardly manner . . . there was a general melée, blows were struck and the utmost excitement prevailed.'[111]

Someone grabbed hold of Herbert Gear between the legs. In trying to free himself, he 'fell into the arms of other roughs.' They chased him down Wote Street and caught up with him by the Countess of Huntingdon's chapel. They grabbed hold of him from behind by his coat, arm and hair. Edward Paget tried to rescue him, so the gang turned on Paget instead, punching and kicking him. In the confusion Herbert managed to get away. He struggled as far as James Webb's house before the gang caught up with him. They pushed him half way over some spiked wooden railings in front of Mr Webb's house and beat him over the head with sticks. Mr Webb and his son heard Herbert's screams, and rushed out to rescue him. James Webb said:

> I have no doubt that had he not been taken into my house, he would have been so exhausted in a few minutes that he would have dropped down and in all probability would have been killed. He was bleeding at the mouth when we took him in, and was very weak.[112]

Meanwhile, the rest of the Salvation Army tried to form a procession down Church Street by linking arms. Superintendent Hibberd and Sergeant Waldren kept separating them, only for them to link arms again

109   *War Cry*, 9 March 1882.
110   TNA PRO HO 45/9607/A2886.
111   *War Cry*, 9 March 1882.
112   TNA PRO HO 45/9607/A2886.

in defiance of the Order of 14 February. When they got to the bottom of Church Street, by the bridge over the Loddon, the Massaganians tried to push Captain Fenny into the river. Probably for the Captain's own safety, Councillor Knight told Superintendent Hibberd to lock Fenny up. Seeing this, some of the Massagainians shouted, 'Bravo, Mr Knight!' The next thing witnesses saw was Captain Fenny being marched towards New Street Police Station between two policemen. Captain Fenny was released about an hour later without charge.

When the Army had almost reached their factory, they were once again set upon by the Massagainians, who pushed several of their number into the muddy brook that used to run parallel with Brook Street. George Woodman said that the Massagainians ducked six Salvation Army lassies in the ditch. They knocked other Salvationists down and trampled them in the mud. Eli Duffin said the Massagainians pushed him and hustled him about, till he was forced into the stream, 'and when there, they tried to get my head under the surface.' One poor woman (Eli's wife, Ellen) after having been thrown into the stream, fell into a dead faint and was carried into the factory by a doctor who happened to be present.[113] However, the *Gazette* noted:

> One of the members of the Army (a cripple) received the kindest protection from one of the leaders of the mob (Barkham). The latter offered to conduct the former safely to the factory. The offer was accepted, and the soldier, with his arm round the neck of his temporary friend, was duly conveyed to his destination according to contract.[114]

As well as the *Pall Mall Gazette*'s report of the disturbance (see beginning of this chapter), other national papers printed similar stories, including the *Graphic* and *Reynolds News*. The *War Cry* commented:

> When the publicans became conscious of what effect the Army work was having on their trade, they began to organise the opposition, and the one end they have in view is to drive them out of the town. Unfortunately during that year, the Mayor was a publican [*sic*], owning three-quarters of the public houses in the town, and who, throughout, has winked at the rowdyism. Consequently, the baser sort have had every encouragement to persist in their attacks, and the law has become a terror, not to evil doers, but to those who do well.[115]

113   Ibid.
114   *Hants and Berks Gazette*, 11 March 1882.
115   *War Cry*, 9 March 1882.

'BARBAROUS BASINGSTOKE'

On 7 March 1882 the magistrates met and proposed that Messrs Knight and Kingdon should prepare a statement of 'the affairs of Sunday last' for George Sclater Booth, and that Mr Sclater Booth be requested to ask the Home Secretary what they should do if the Salvation Army gave notice of parading the streets again.

On the 9th Richard Knight reported back to the magistrates. He told them that, while in London, he and Mr Kingdon had visited General Booth. Booth insisted on a constitutional right of procession in the face of the proclamation, but, in order to prevent any future disturbances, he accepted the offer of using Mr Blatch's meadow for their open air meetings provided that the Army was fully protected by the police. He would also tell Captain Fenny not to sing when they were marching to and from the meadow. During the interview General Booth complained about the conduct of the Borough Police and said that he intended to have a question raised in Parliament about the Basingstoke disturbances.

When the two magistrates saw Mr Sclater Booth and William Beach, the two Members for North Hampshire, the MPs strongly advised the magistrates not to raise a question with the Home Secretary. The Home Secretary was 'convinced that the publicans of the town supported the rough element and that they thought his reply would be somewhat injurious to the town.' The MPs said that if it was proved that the Borough Police could not suppress any disturbances, the magistrates should substitute the County Police in their place.[116]

General Booth's question in Parliament was raised by W. S. Caine, MP for Barrow-in-Furness. On 16 March 1882 he asked the Home Secretary:

> If he has received a Memorial, accompanied by sworn information, from several of the leading tradesmen of Basingstoke, with regard to the riots which have taken place in that town recently, and at recurring intervals during the last twelve months, caused by the persistent efforts of an organised gang of roughs to suppress by violence and intimidation the processions and meetings of a religious body known as the 'Salvation Army'; whether he has instituted any inquiry, with a view of ascertaining the names and position of those

---

116   Minutes of the Basingstoke Petty Court, 1881–3.

who are well known to be the ringleaders of this dangerous mob; and, if he will take prompt and immediate steps to secure for the 'Salvation Army' that protection from injury and outrage which the magistrates and police of Basingstoke do not afford them?

Sir William Harcourt replied that he had no power to direct the magistrates. They had the responsibility to preserve the peace as they thought fit.

Now, as respects Basingstoke, there were great disturbances this time last year. The Mayor and magistrates did what was very proper. There being these processions of the 'Salvation Army' attacked by the mob, they made every effort to protect the 'Army'. They had out their own constables, which were, I believe, 16 in number, and swore in 100 special constables, and had, besides, a detachment of Artillery. Then the magistrates, expecting the thing would happen again, came to me, and said, what was very reasonable, that they could not expect to have a detachment of Artillery every Sunday, and that special constables, with their best clothes on ready for going to church, did not want to fight with the mob on Sunday. They asked me what, under the circumstances, I would advise them to do . . . I wrote the letter, which has always been written for several years, applicable to those circumstances . . . Having accepted the advice contained in the letter, they issued a proclamation forbidding the procession, and peace was preserved in Basingstoke from April to August. But a change took place, either in the personnel or the opinions of the Bench. They disregarded the advice I had tendered, and withdrew the proclamation. [Mr. SCLATER-BOOTH: No, no.] Well, I beg pardon. The right hon. Gentleman says 'No'; but I had my information from the Mayor, who, finding there was a majority against him, no longer issued the proclamation, and, therefore, a disturbance took place. The consequence was that there had been disturbances ever since . . . It is not in my power to compel the magistrates to do what they do not see fit to do. If they do not preserve the peace they are liable to a criminal information for failing to do their duty . . . I may say that those people cannot be too strongly condemned who attack persons who are only meeting for a lawful and, I may say, laudable object; but, on the other hand, I cannot but condemn the imprudence of those who encourage these processions, which experience has shown must lead to disorder and violence.[117]

---

117   House of Commons Debates *16 March 1882* vol. 267 cols 989–91.

(The Borough had only five constables. The Home Secretary may have been including constables borrowed from the County Police.)

Basingstoke's reputation suffered further damage when there was a riot in the Corn Exchange that made the national press. The *Echo* wrote:

> About midway between London and Salisbury there is a benighted little town which appears to be inhabited chiefly by a race of barbarians, somewhat similar to those who are described in the traveller's note book thus:- 'Manners none; customs beastly.' These people pelt, beat and kick men and women whose only offence is that they sing hymns in the open air; they treat a minister of religion in like manner because he has sought to protect their victims; they stone the windows of a magistrate because he has had the courage to maintain the law; and when their proceedings have become so outrageous that fourteen of the worst are sent to prison, a public banquet, terminating in a drunken orgy and riot, is given to them on their release . . . But can nothing be done for Barbarous Basingstoke? Cannot the Church Missionary Society open a special fund to send a missionary to bring this dark spot within the pale of Christian civilisation?[118]

Once again our old friend W. S .Caine raised a question in the House. He asked the Home Secretary:

> If his attention has been called to a paragraph in the 'Daily News' of yesterday, headed 'Uproarious Meeting at Basingstoke,' describing a meeting held by Mr. Arch in that town, in the Corn Exchange, to consider the question of the agricultural labourer. It states that—
> The room was occupied before the proceedings commenced by a gang of roughs. Mr. Arch attempted to speak, but was refused a hearing, and was pelted with rotten eggs and ochre. Mr. Mitchell shared the same fate. After an hour and a half had been vainly spent in endeavouring to obtain quietude, the meeting was brought to an end amid much uproar; whether the authorities of Basingstoke were aware that this meeting was broken up by the same organized gang whose violence towards the members of the Salvation Army has more than once been the subject of Parliamentary inquiry; and, if the Home Office will take the matter into immediate consideration?

(Joseph Arch and George Mitchell were leaders of the National Agricultural Workers Union.)

Caine's colleague, Sir Wilfred Lawson, MP for Carlisle, asked the Home Secretary:

---

118   *Echo*, 12 March 1882.

Whether it is true that, on September 21st 1881, ten of the Basingstoke roughs were released from Winchester Gaol, where they had been suffering a fortnight's imprisonment for attacks on the Salvation Army; whether they were brought home to Basingstoke in a carriage and four, escorted by outriders in fancy costumes, and accompanied by their supporters, the brewers and publicans of Basingstoke; whether, in the evening, a banquet was given to the released prisoners in the Corn Exchange, which was granted for the purpose by the Corporation, the proceedings being wound up by a free fight, in which the police were powerless; and, whether any communication has been made from the Home Office to the authorities of Basingstoke, with a view to the better preservation of order?

The Home Secretary replied that the local authority had not drawn either of those two incidents to his attention.[119]

At a subsequent meeting of the Town Council, the Council were asked to approve the payment of £14 7s 3d for the Magistrates' visits to London. Alderman Allen objected to the payment. He said that the journeys were unnecessary. He contended that the instructions received from the Home Secretary were so definite there was no need for such visits. They should have dispersed the Army as they were ordered to do: and if they met in five or six places, they knew where to get the desired number of police to do the work. He thought it was rather derogatory to visit General Booth, 'They might as well go and visit Captain Barkham.'

Ex-Mayor Blatch said that he took credit to himself and his fellow magistrates for having gone to the Home Office instead of acting on their own responsibility. It was a consolation to know that Sir William Harcourt had said in the House that 'the Mayor and the magistrates had acted very properly.' He said they could congratulate themselves that they were not now in the position of Mr Melville Portal.[120] (Portal was Chairman of the Overton magistrates who sentenced four members of the Salvation Army to a month's hard labour for persisting in a procession at Whitchurch. The Salvation Army appealed to the Court of Queen's Bench, who quashed the conviction and ordered the magistrates to pay all the expenses of the application.)

After the Salvation Army started using ex-Mayor Blatch's Meadow for their open air meetings with police protection, things quietened down for a bit. There were isolated incidents, however. On 9 April 1882, when the Salvation Army were carrying their stools back to their barracks from the

119   House of Commons Debates *16 March 1882* vol. *267 cols 1016-7*.
120   *Hants and Berks Gazette*, 6 May 1882.

Albert Lansley (Jean Willoughby)

meadow, Albert Lansley attacked David Smith. Lansley claimed that he lashed out at Smith because Smith had hit him in the face with his stool. However, Superintendent Hibberd, who witnessed the affair, confirmed that this was an unprovoked attack by Lansley. When Hibberd arrested him and tried to take him to the Police Station, some of his friends attempted a rescue. Hibberd had to call on bystanders to assist him in the name of the Queen and on the way to the Police Station, William Bryant hit one of the people helping. In order to show that they would come down hard on those who interfered with the Salvation Army while they kept to their agreement not to hold processions through the town, the magistrates sentenced Lansley to one month's hard labour, and William Bryant got seven days'.[121]

While Lansley was serving his sentence, the following handbill was circulated around town:

> This is Salvation again – To all who sympathise with the poor boy Albert Lansley, seventeen years of age, now serving one month's hard labour in Winchester Gaol, through what is called the Salvation Army, to which he had really done no harm. We wish to get up a subscription to make him a suitable present on his return, which the Committee may think most suitable, for the suffering he has undergone which never would have happened had the Salvation Army never entered our quiet town and made hundreds of families miserable. The subscription will be limited from 2d to 6d. If we are to give the boy a good reception here, it will be the means of lifting up a respectable tradesman's family of thirteen, and we all know what a sad blow it must be to the father and mother. It is therefore

121 Minutes of the Basingstoke Petty Court, 1881–3.

hoped that there will be a liberal response to the appeal.

Donations will be received by W Lansley, London Street, Basingstoke.

W. Lansley would have been Walter Lansley, Albert's older brother. They both worked as farriers in their father John's Veterinary Forge in London Street. It is not known what response his appeal achieved.

Captain Fenny decided to take his message to the villagers of Up Nately on 1 May. The Salvation Army and their followers held a service in a meadow belonging to a Mr Goddard (not the Mr Goddard who charged his horse and cart through the Salvation Army meeting in August 1881). Shortly after the service began, 'a gang of roughs from Basingstoke and neighbourhood' arrived and kept up a 'continual fire of blasphemy'. When the service was over, the soldiers and their sympathisers made for the building where it was intended to hold their evening service. During the course of their journey, someone threw a turnip at Captain Fenny that gave him a severe blow to the back of the head. According to George Woodman, Captain Fenny was also thrown in the river.

Once the Salvationists reached the building, the opposition contented themselves with standing outside, making as much noise as possible. Bored with this, they decided to invade the building. 'This caused sufficient commotion and fear by their shameful oaths to completely break up the meeting.' Captain Fenny was escorted to Mr Goddard's house for his own safety, where he remained until nearly midnight when it was considered it was safe for him to go home. Even so, he had to be accompanied all the way home by a policeman.[122]

On 4 June 1882, a gang of 50 or 60 people were milling around outside the barracks, obstructing the doorway as the Salvation Army were returning from Blatch's Meadow. When PC Pearce tried to clear a passage, William Jones, William Lambden, Charles Pranknell and Joseph Ilsley refused to move and 'made use of bad language'. They surrounded Pearce and started 'pushing and hustling' him. Lambden held his fist in Pearce's face, while one of the other three shouted, 'Hit him'. Fortunately for Lambden, he declined, as the punishment for hitting a policeman could have been severe. All four were fined £2 each with 3s 6d costs or one month's hard labour in default.[123]

In the evening of Saturday 29 July 1882, the Salvation Army tried to hold an open air service in the Market Place. About 100 people were present – the usual mix of supporters and Massagainians. Ernest Fitzgerald, Charles Castle, Charles Hine, and the Barkham brothers were 'carrying on an opposition'. William Phillips the labourer (as opposed to William

---

122   Quotations taken from the *Hants and Berks Gazette*, 6 May 1882.
123   Minutes of the Basingstoke Petty Court, 1881–3.

Phillips the blacksmith, who appears later), was singing and dancing in the middle of the ring formed by the Salvation Army. While the Army were trying to pray, he treated them to a rendition of the song, 'The Union Jack of Old England'.

The Salvation Army abandoned their service and began to march down Wote Street. The Massagainians charged down the hill after them, pushing them onto the pavement to get in front. During the scuffles, Harry Barkham alleged that George McManus, a Salvationist, had hit him with his stick. Superintendent Hibberd later told the Court:

> Fitzgerald said that it was 'a bloody unlawful weapon to have in his hand. He ought not to have it.' I told Fitzgerald to go away and be quiet and that McManus had a right to his stick as he was doing no harm with it. Fitzgerald said he would 'knock his bloody ear with it' and seized the stick and took it out of his hand. McManus had a crack on his head. I heard it rattle. I don't know who gave him the blow, but I think Fitzgerald. I saw the stick in the hand of someone and I snatched and took possession of it. Castle took off his coat and offered to fight any bugger and if he began he would sweep the lot. Their conduct was very bad . . . Fitzgerald was swearing and using bad language . . . They left together and made a tumult down Wote Street. When we got to Brook Street, Phillips the blacksmith and Thomas Powell appeared. William Phillips the blacksmith was walking backwards and forwards, knocking up against people and saying 'Make room for me'.

According to Sergeant Waldren's testimony, when Phillips was told to go away, he continued walking backwards and forwards saying, 'I'm a–moving; I'm a–moving' and he would 'bloody well go when he liked.'

When Superintendent Hibberd told them they were causing an obstruction and he would summons them, Castle pulled off his coat again and threw it on the ground. He said he would, 'fight any bugger who was there'. According to Sergeant Waldren:

> He looked into the Superintendent's face and said, 'I don't care a fuck though there are two of you there.' I then told Castle he had better go away. Powell and Hine took hold of him. Phillips the blacksmith picked up his coat. Fitzgerald continued swearing. His oaths were very bad.

His mates took Castle to the *Railway Arms* to continue their Saturday night's drinking.[124]

---

124   Ibid.

When the case came to court on 8 August, Charles Castle, Harry and Frank Barkham, the two William Phillips, Henry Rawlings, Charles Hine, Thomas Powell, and Ernest Fitzgerald were charged with 'having on the 29th July, unlawfully obstructed the free passage of a highway called Wote-street by assembling, with others, to the number of one hundred persons or thereabouts.'

Frank Barkham was absent at the camp at Sandhurst, and Phillips the labourer and Rawlings had absconded. The remaining defendants attended the court, but were drunk and kept interrupting the evidence. Castle was 'so loud and demonstrative' in his cross-examination of Sergeant Waldren that he had to be forcibly ejected from the court room.

When the magistrates retired to consider their verdict:

> . . . a scene occurred very similar to that which might be expected in a public-house tap-room on a Saturday evening. Many shouted out in high tones remarks which were excessively indecent, and these were laughed at and loudly applauded. The production and consumption of a bottle of beer by the defendant Powell, who was making himself comfortable at full length in one of the town-hall chairs, was the cause of much laughter among his companions in court. Most of the defendants had evidently been drinking to excess, and Fitzgerald, who was more intoxicated than the rest, was most uproarious in his behaviour. He first treated the company to the solo, 'The Salvation Army Will Be There', to their evident delight, and then walking over to the superintendent of police (who was sitting in his chair) he commenced using language of an abusive and threatening character. When ordered to desist he struck the Supt one or two blows on the shoulder. Supt Hibberd now rose from his chair, thrust the offender aside, and ordered him to be removed from the court. This order was speedily carried out by Sergeant Waldren and PC Trodd, who met with considerable resistance in the shape of kicks and struggles . . . [When the Magistrates returned they fined Fitzgerald and Castle 10 shillings each for bad language, and Frank and Harry Barkham, Phillips the labourer, Castle and Fitzgerald 10 shillings and costs for obstructing the highway. Only three of the defendants were in court to hear the verdict _ the others had gone out for more beer. When they returned] . . . Fitzgerald appeared more intoxicated than ever, being scarcely able to stand. On being told that he would have to pay 35s, he said he should not do so. The default was three weeks' hard labour, and the sergeant was about to remove him to the police station when Fitzgerald commenced a terrible resistance. He threatened in a loud voice to kick the constables' jaws out, and he would have doubtless have striven

to carry this threat into execution had he not been thrown to the ground and held down by four constables. In this struggle Fitzgerald kicked the back of a chair off. PC Hurst placed the handcuffs on him, and a slip, used for the purpose of tying a prisoner's feet together to prevent him from kicking, was fastened round his legs. He was placed on a form and held down while a stretcher was fetched from the police station. In the meantime he called loudly to be released, and when a fall of glass was heard on the pavement outside the Town-hall, he cried, 'That's it, smash the b— windows'. The stretcher having now been brought, the prisoner's boots were removed . . . he was placed on the stretcher, safely strapped down, and conveyed to the station, accompanied by a crowd composed partly of sympathisers with the prisoner. Sergeant Waldren had the honour of taking the front part of the stretcher, and the prisoner gratified his revenge by tugging at the sergeant's coat tail, and declaring that he would tear it to pieces.[125]

During the remainder of 1882 there was very little trouble concerning the Salvation Army; certainly nothing that was brought to the attention of the borough magistrates. There was the occasional complaint in the papers about youths throwing mud at the Salvationists outside the factory and disrupting the meetings inside the factory by shouting 'Alleluia' and 'Praise the Lord' at inappropriate intervals during the service, and perhaps getting a fit of the giggles while doing so.

The Municipal Election in November passed off quietly. Also in November Mayor Lodwidge's term of office was over, and F. J. Temple was elected in his stead and took his place as Chief Magistrate; and PC Trodd was promoted to Sergeant following the death of Sergeant Waldren (see Appendix 1).

---

125   *Hants and Berks Gazette*, 12 August 1882.

1883: THE BEGINNING OF THE END

The low level harassment of the Salvation Army continued into the New Year, but the opposition mainly came from teenagers seeking entertainment on the otherwise boring Basingstoke Sundays. A nasty incident took place at the start of the year when 14-year-old Thomas Bartlett, alias Bradfield, and 18-year-old Mark Harfield were found guilty of indecently assaulting two girls as they left the Salvation Army meeting on 7 January 1883. The two lads were sentenced to 14 days' hard labour.

On 22 April Bartlett was in trouble again, for striking Eli Duffin as Duffin was trying persuade Bartlett to leave the factory. When Duffin was walking home, Bartlett hit him again. When the case came to court on 1 May, Mayor Temple said:

> There is no doubt an assault has been committed, and you will be fined, including costs, 10s 6d. You ought not to have been there making a noise and assaulting people, and such conduct will not be allowed. In default of payment you will go to Winchester gaol for 14 days' hard labour.[126]

Around midnight on the night of 2 May 1883 a group of youths, including Edward Jeffreys and Charles Pranknell, were hanging around in Flaxfield Road. Egged on by the others, Charles Pranknell threw a brick through Daniel Goodall's bedroom window, much to the surprise of Mr and Mrs Goodall, who were in bed at the time. Pranknell was fined 14 shillings, plus 2 shillings for the repair of the window.

Edward Jeffreys appears again when Superintendent Hibberd summonsed him for wilfully loitering on the highway in Brook Street on 22 July and refusing to move when requested. He was with a crowd of 30 or 40 'being directly in front of the door [of the Salvation Army factory] wringing his fists in a fighting manner against Goodall the doorkeeper.'

There were only two incidents in 1883 that involved some of the original Massagainians. The first was on Monday 19 February 1883. This is what Sergeant Trodd told the magistrates:

> About 7.30 I heard a great noise and shouting at the bottom of Flaxfield. When I arrived I found the Salvation Army had formed

---

a ring and Frank Barkham and another man linked together were dancing round in the middle of it. They were pushing everyone who came near and shouting. I called on them to desist. They were like two madmen. After, I called on the leader of the Salvation Army not to preach, fearing a great disturbance. Barkham and the other man tried all they could to prevent the Salvation Army from starting. He continued pushing people about all up the hill. He was very drunk. He took no notice of anything I said to him.

Superintendent Hibberd continued the story:

On Monday 19th I was on duty in Church Street. I saw the defendant there. There was one each side of him and had hold of him apparently leading him. I followed them down the street. They were making a hideous noise, groaning and shouting and they kept this up round Brook Street by the Factory though Essex Road. Barkham was making a great noise. He was fearfully drunk and must have fallen had he not been held up.[127]

Barkham was fined five shillings and 9s 6d costs, with 14 days' hard labour in default.

The second incident took place on 27 May and was reported by Lieutenant William Kerr in the *War Cry* as follows:

We went to the Market Place and had a short stand. We were surrounded by a large number of the devil's servants, who commenced pushing the sisters and using the most frightful language. We formed a procession again to go back to our hall, but had not marched far when some of these young men, headed by a publican, blocked the road so that we could not proceed. Then they commenced to abuse the Soldiers, knocking them about – brothers and sisters shared alike. Two of our noble soldiers were knocked down, and then kicked about. Some of our sisters were used so badly that they were not fit to work next morning. This continued for a long time, and not one policeman could be seen.[128]

The *Hants and Berks Gazette* missed the excitement. On 2 June it reported:

A serious disturbance took place during the procession of the Salvation Army, the particulars of which, in the absence of our reporter, have been furnished by 'one who was there' as follows:-
    I desire to call your attention to the scandalous treatment which the soldiers of the Salvation Army received from a howling mob of

127 Minutes of the Basingstoke Petty Court, 1881–3.
128 *War Cry*, 9 June 1883.

some 200 young men on Sunday afternoon. The open-air procession started as usual from the factory, shortly after two o'clock and marched directly to the Market-place, where the members held a short service. These young men then gathered round and behaved themselves in a most disgraceful manner, and used the most obscene language. After stopping here for about ten minutes, the procession again started for the factory. A short distance down Wote-street, these young men blocked up the roadway so that the procession came to a standstill, and then the real fighting commenced. The mob broke into the procession, pushed the Army soldiers about, knocked two of them down, and kicked them in a most brutal manner. One of them, by the way, was a woman. The women were knocked about like footballs. This continued for over half an hour. One policeman only turned up, and he was helpless. The mob, who had a publican at their head, acted like brute beasts.

The story of the events of 27 May emerged when Frank and Harry Barkham, Henry Jeffrey, Charles Pranknell, Charles Porter alias Price, and Alfred Jennings appeared before the magistrates on 5 June charged with 'obstructing the free passage of Wote-street by assembling therein with others to the number of a hundred or thereabouts.'

PC Eales gave evidence that the Salvation Army were parading down Wote Street at about 2.30 p.m. The six defendants were in front of them and stopped abruptly in front of Mr Knight's house, blocking the road. He asked them to move on, but they refused. There were about 26 Salvation Army soldiers and there were about 200 persons accompanying them. PC Eales explained that he had been in the police force for only nine months, and he made the selection of the six defendants because he knew them well and they appeared to be the ringleaders. But the implication from his evidence, and that of the other witnesses was that, as in so many of the incidents since the Salvation Army came to Basingstoke, those who were summonsed before the magistrates were just a small sample of those who were involved in the disturbances.

When the procession was stopped, PC Eales said he heard one of the defendants say, 'Don't push me', and then fighting commenced. It appears that George Doswell, who was in the front rank of the Army, cannoned into one of those who were obstructing the procession. Someone started pushing him about and hit him in the face. Alfred Jennings pushed him against a wall and both Jennings and Charles Porter hit him. George's cousin, William Doswell, said that 'had not I and others not gone to his assistance, they would, I believe, have killed him. They were like wild men.'

The Massagainians broke up the procession and continued pushing the Salvationists around until they reached the Wharf Gates, where the defendants and others blocked the road in a V formation. Someone grabbed hold of Lieutenant Kerr and a cry rang out of 'Let's throw the buggers in the river.' Lieutenant Kerr said that he was 'knocked about a good deal. Some were so badly used; so much so that they were unable to go to work the next morning.'

The Mayor fined each of the defendants five shillings and 5s 6d costs and added that if any of those cases were again brought before them, they would be dealt with more severely. Some of the defendants paid at once. Others asked for time to pay, and were allowed a week, with the exception of Charles Porter, whose application was opposed by Superintendent Hibberd, who described Porter as 'a bird of passage'. George Brown of the *Royal Exchange* settled the question by paying his fine.[129]

The identity of the publican referred to in the *War Cry* and the *Gazette* reports became clear when the annual licences came up for renewal by the Borough magistrates on 20 August. When John Moger's licence for the *Jolly Farmer*, Bunnian Place was being considered, Superintendent Hibberd told the Magistrates that, 'on one occasion in a semi-state of drunkenness, he led a party of ignorant boys to break the peace of the town by following up the Salvation Army. He had done this for several week nights, but this was particularly noticeable one Sunday.' Moger apologised for his actions and said it would not happen again. His licence was renewed.

In September 1883 the Salvation Army moved from the factory to their new premises in Reading Road. Catherine Booth conducted the opening service. During the service someone threw a large flint stone through the skylight, showering the congregation with glass. She told the congregation not to look up, and the rest of the service continued without incident.[130]

The last attack on the Salvation Army I can find appears to have been an isolated, spur of the moment affair that was reported in the *Hants and Berks Gazette* for 13 October 1883 as follows:

WHAT A BOON!

James Boon, a middle-aged man, of unhandsome appearance, stood before the Bench, and with downcast head muttered his admission of the offence of being drunk and disorderly in the Reading-road on the previous evening.

Sergeant Trodd, in stating the facts, said: About half-past nine last night I was fetched to the new Salvation Barracks. When I got there prisoner Boon had left the barracks and gone into the *Waggon and Horses* opposite. The landlady, who was trying to get him out,

---

129   *Hants and Berks Gazette*, 9 June 1883 and Minutes of the Basingstoke Petty Court, 1881–3.

130   Clements, Ken, *Two Feeble Women: The Early History of the Salvation Army in Basingstoke* (no publisher noted, *c.* 1995).

The Salvation Army's new hall in Reading Road (Robert Brown)

called me in, and I put him in the street. He walked, or rather, staggered, down the road and turned towards Basing, but he shortly came back into the Reading-road and met several members of the Army. On getting near them he struck the captain a deliberate blow in the face. He was very drunk and I took him into custody.

Prisoner was further charged with assaulting Thomas Poulter, a member of the Army, at the same time and place. To this also he pleaded guilty.

Complainant said he was in the Salvation Barracks and while there he heard several stones come up on the building. He went out to see who it was flinging, and saw several parties who affirmed it was Boon. To Boon, who had a thick short stick in his hand, witness said, 'Good-evening', to which the prisoner responded by making at him with the stick. Witness received a blow in the face, and said to the prisoner, 'You might have blinded me with that stick'. Prisoner then aimed another blow at witness's head, and sent his hat flying across the road. Prisoner was drunk, but seemed to thoroughly understand what he was about. He could comprehend very well what was said to him.

The Captain of the Army, Alfred Reynolds, also preferred a similar charge against the prisoner, who again admitted his guilt. The captain said he left the barracks after the meeting was closed, and he had bade his friends 'Good-night', and on his way down the road he met James Boon. He asked Boon why he came to meetings and disturbed them. Why didn't he stop away? Boon said, 'Who are you?' and there deliberately struck witness in the jaw with his fist.

Prisoner said if he had not been drunk it would not have occurred.

In reply to Mr Wallis: Supt Hibberd said the prisoner had been

up before. He was convicted at this court in 1872, being fined 10s
for being drunk and disorderly; in 1874 he was committed for two
months' hard labour for assault; in 1876 he was committed under the
bye laws for abusive language, and sentenced to fourteen days, and
he has been convicted at other courts since then.

The Mayor (to prisoner): You have been here before us three
or four times, but it does not seem to have any effect on you, and
therefore we will punish you severely. You will be sent to Winchester
for two months' hard labour.

After the case was over, Captain Reynolds asked whether something
could be done to protect the new barracks. He complained that, since the
new barracks had been opened, the lock had been broken off the gate, the
windows had been broken, one of the piers had been damaged, the top
stone broken off, some bricks and mortar had been removed, and the flag
had been stolen right from the top of the building. (Someone later reported
seeing it flying from a tree at Winslade.[131]) The Magistrates patiently
explained that, with only five constables at their command, they could not
expect to have a constable stationed outside the barracks every night.

However, there seem to have been no major disturbances against the
Salvation Army in Basingstoke after 1883. I can find no record of the Order
of 14 February 1882 being withdrawn, but the Salvation Army resumed its
processions, and there does not appear to have been any significant disrup-
tion. When Captain Coles left Basingstoke in August 1884 after seven
months to take charge of the Salvation Army corps in Portsmouth, the
Gazette commented:

We are glad to record that during the period in which Captain
Coles has had the command, no disturbances have taken place in
connection with the Army operations which had rendered any action
on the part of the police necessary, and with the exception that
occasionally a few straggling boys have accompanied the soldiers
on their route, and mingled a few inharmonious shouts with theirs,
there has been nothing of which complaint would be made. After the
painful experience of the past every resident must feel heartily glad.[132]

The only case that came before the Basingstoke magistrates concerning
the Salvation Army in the years after 1883 was that of Henry Powell and
William Mudge, two boys who were caught throwing clods of earth at the
Salvation Army building in November 1884.[133]

131   Clements, Ken, *Two Feeble Women: The Early History of the Salvation Army
in Basingstoke* (no publisher noted, *c.* 1995).
132   *Hants and Berks Gazette*, 2 August 1884.
133   Minutes of the Basingstoke Petty Court 1883–6.

WHERE BASINGSTOKE LEADS, OTHERS FOLLOW*

With apologies to Manchester

Why should miserable little towns in the south of England show themselves so restive under the visitation of the Salvation Army? In the north and in great centres of population General Booth's troops parade and drum and sing to their hearts' content without interference. But at Basingstoke, Guildford, and now at Worthing, the mob is continually maltreating the processionists, and indulging in that which culminated last night in Worthing in the sacking of a tradesman's house and the reading of the Riot Act.

Pall Mall Gazette, 21 August 1884

Basingstoke was not the first place to riot against the Salvation Army. The earliest incidents were in the East End of London. But Basingstoke was one of the earliest, and it was Basingstoke that captured the attention of Parliament and the press; and perhaps provided the inspiration for riots elsewhere. After the March 1881 riots, there were disturbances in at least 60 other towns and cities, mainly between 1882 and 1884.[134] William Booth claimed that 669 Salvationists, 251 of whom were women, were injured and 56 buildings damaged in 1882 alone.[135] Sporadic riots against the Salvation Army continued through the 1880s and into the early 1890s, notably the Eastbourne riots of 1891.[136]

Towards the end of 1881, the Salvation Army in Weston-super-Mare were attacked by a group calling themselves the Skeleton Army. The opposition in other towns adopted that title, although it never took off in Basingstoke. In Honiton, the Skeleton Army even produced its own newspaper, *The Skeleton*, which parodied the military language of the *War Cry*. It described its troops as undertaking exercises, 'including throwing turnips, artistic decoration with red ochre, and turf planting.'[137] When the turnip season was over, the resourceful Honiton brigade turned to cow

---

134   Bailey, Victor, 'Salvation Army Riots, the Salvation Army and Legal Authority in the Provincial Town', in A. P. Donajgrodski (ed.) *Social Control in Nineteenth Century Britain* (Croom Helm, 1977).

135   Hattersley, Roy, *Blood and Fire: William and Catherine Booth and their Salvation Army* (Little, Brown, 1999).

136   Walker, Pamela J., *Pulling the Devil's Kingdom Down: The Salvation Army in Victorian Britain* (University of California, 2001).

137   Ibid.

dung as their missile of choice. On one occasion the Honiton skeletons snatched the musical instruments away from the Salvation Army band, stamped on them and kicked them round the streets.[138]

The Frome division of the Skeleton Army undertook a similar exercise in musical destruction when they battered the Salvation Army's instruments out of shape and cut the skin of the big bass drum.[139] When the Salvation Army were banging their drum outside John Roe's brewery in Whitchurch in April 1884, while his youngest child was seriously ill with bronchitis and congestion of the brain, Roe came storming out, armed with a clasp knife and slashed the skin of the drum.[140]

In Salisbury a crowd of around 1,000 skeletons threw rotten eggs, bags of flour and fireworks at a Salvation Army procession, 'to the serious injury of many'.[141] In Ryde a group of Hallelujah Lasses were showered with liquid manure and sewer contents.[142] The Crediton brigade of the Skeleton Army ambushed a band of Salvationists travelling in a carriage, cut the reins, loosened a wheel and sent the carriage and its occupants hurtling down a hill.[143]

With the exception of a few isolated incidents, such as a riot during the Salvation Army's Annual Council of War in Sheffield in January 1882, the towns and cities of the industrial North were less affected by Salvation Army disturbances. This was probably due to a combination of the strong tradition of working class non-conformity and the existence of large police forces.

Most of the riots took place in the smaller towns and cities in Southern England and the Home Counties where the rioters were seen by some local authorities as defending the economic interests of their town, whether in brewery towns like Basingstoke and Whitchurch, or in seaside towns and health resorts where there was middle class concern that noisy bands and processions would deter visitors who came for peace and quiet and would ruin the trade of the town. There were complaints that Salvation Army processions were inconveniencing the peaceable inhabitants when they were setting off to their respective places of worship. Skeleton Armies were particularly active in cathedral cities like Exeter and Salisbury, and in resorts like Weston-super-Mare, Worthing, Eastbourne, Brighton,

---

138   *Pall Mall Gazette*, 20 November, 1882.

139   *The Times*, 30 August 1884.

140   Smith, Martin, *The Salvation Army Disturbances in Whitchurch 1881–1890* (no publisher noted).

141   House of Commons Debates, 14 July 1882, vol.272 col.447.

142   *Ryde and Isle of Wight News*, 24 September 1886.

143   Bailey, Victor, 'Salvation Army Riots, the Salvation Army and Legal Authority in the Provincial Town', in A. P. Donajgrodski (ed.) *Social Control in Nineteenth Century Britain* (Croom Helm, 1977).

Folkestone and Tunbridge Wells, places one would not associate with street battles and rioting.

Many places with limited police numbers followed Basingstoke's lead in trying to maintain the peace of the town by banning Salvation Army processions and outdoor meetings. However, the landmark case of Beatty v Gillbanks took this weapon away. Following a series of violent clashes between the Skeleton and the Salvation Armies in the streets of Weston-super-Mare, the local magistrates issued an Order banning processions. In defiance of the Order, Captain Beatty led a procession of 'one hundred or more persons' and refused to disperse when ordered to do so by the police. He was arrested and bound over to keep the peace, and in default to be imprisoned for three months. This provided the Salvation Army with the test case the Basingstoke police and magistrates had denied them. The Salvation Army appealed to the High Court. In June 1882 Mr Justice Field ruled that there was no authority for the contention 'that a man may be convicted for doing a lawful act if he knows that his doing it may cause another to do an unlawful act.'

This completely reversed the advice that successive Home Secretaries since 1865 had given magistrates in Basingstoke and elsewhere. Therefore, even if the magistrates had reason to suppose that Salvation Army processions would incite others to commit a breach of the peace, they could no longer ban them for fear of expensive legal challenge.

After Beatty v Gillbanks, magistrates could only fall back on trying to maintain order by augmenting their police forces by creating special constables or borrowing policemen from other forces, at a cost to their ratepayers; or by arresting Salvationists for obstructing the highway. This last option was taken away by a ruling concerning the Salvation Army in Whitchurch.

The Whitchurch corps of the Salvation Army used to hold short services in the Town Square, where the Basingstoke to Andover road meets the Winchester to Newbury road. There was a series of arrests for unlawful assembly and obstruction of the highway. In each case, the Salvationists refused to pay their fines and were sent to prison. In 1889 the Salvation Army appealed to the High Court. Lord Justice Coleridge ruled that a mere temporary inconvenience was not an indictable offence if the meetings did not cause a real and substantial obstruction of the highway.[144] This ruling, and Beatty v Gillbanks, were significant advances in the freedom of assembly, for which demonstrators of all shades of opinion have the Salvation Army to thank.

---

144   Smith, Martin, *The Salvation Army Disturbances in Whitchurch 1881–1890* (no publisher noted).

BASINGSTOKE REUNITED

Why did the riots in Basingstoke end, just at the time they were picking up elsewhere? The straight answer is that we can only surmise. According to George Woodman, writing about the Massagainians in 1930:

> The decision of the Lord Chief Justice with regard to the imprisonment of Salvationists at Whitchurch and the decision in favour of Salvationists at Weston super Mare seems to have silenced them forever. They were tired out with ill-treating the Salvationists . . . so they went about their work without anyone persecuting the Salvation Army. Some had reason to leave for work elsewhere.[145]

There is probably a degree of truth in Woodman's statement. When the Salvation Army came to Basingstoke and declared that it would 'open fire on Sin and Satan', by which it meant the drinking classes, it was not surprising that that fire was returned with interest. In its early years, the Salvation Army must have seemed to be an awesome organisation: an invading army with an effective national coordination, bringing in officers from all over the country. If its own publicity is to be believed, the Salvation Army actually did have an effect on the profits of the brewers and publicans in the first few months of its arrival.

However, over time, the novelty would have worn off. I suspect that, by the end of 1881, it would already have converted those who, through alcoholic remorse or other reasons, wanted to give up the booze; and that most of those who joined thereafter had probably never even set foot in a pub. After the initial impact, the law of diminishing returns would have set in. What was seen as a threat to the viability of the pubs and breweries, and to the freedom of the drinking classes, never materialised. Indeed, the *Basingstoke Parish Magazine* seems to indicate that in October 1881 the pubs were 'filled as they had never been filled before'.

I think Woodman was correct in saying that the Beatty v Gillbanks decision had an effect. As this rendered the magistrates' Order of 14 February 1882 ineffective, there were no powers to stop the Salvation Army processions without risking an expensive and humiliating defeat in the courts. The alternative was to stop the Massagainians from attacking the Salvationists. If the rioting continued, and Basingstoke's five constables were insufficient to keep the peace, the magistrates would have to bring in the County Police, at a cost to the borough ratepayers.

Towards the end of 1882 it would have been apparent that the Salvation Army was here to stay, and that its processions no longer posed any threat

---

145   *The Rise of the Salvation Army in Basingstoke*, manuscript by George Woodman in the Resource Room of the Willis Museum.

George Woodman, about 1930
(Hampshire County Council Museums & Arts Service)

to the economy of the town. Instead, it would be the Massagainians who would cause the ratepayers to lose money if the riots continued. If, as suggested by the *Hants and Berks Gazette*, the Massagainians were mere hirelings, organised and financed by the Adams brothers, and possibly other brewers behind the scenes, it could be that pressure was applied on the organisers to call their troops off in the ratepayers' interest; or, more likely, that the organisers decided themselves that further Massagainian activity would be pointless.

Edward Adams got married towards the end of 1881 and Valentine Adams in 1883. Both moved out of the brewery; Edward to Devonshire Lodge, and Valentine to a substantial house in Church Street. They had set themselves up as respectable married men, rather than the street fighters of March 1881. In 1884 Edward put himself forward for a seat on the council, and was elected in 1885. He also became a member of the School Board. He probably decided after he got married to disassociate himself from his wild past. It is likely, therefore, that any middle class organisation behind the Massagainian activities had ceased to exist. The isolated incidents that occurred after mid-1882 were spontaneous interludes of high spirits or the work of boys. And even those petered out.

Canon Millard, who was the first signatory on what might be called the 'Massagainian petition', and was the author of the articles in the *Basingstoke Parish Magazine*, eventually came to terms with the existence of

Canon Millard (Hampshire County Council Museums & Arts Service)

the Salvation Army. In 1889 the book he co-authored with Francis Baigent, *A History of the Ancient Town and Manor of Basingstoke*, was published, in which he wrote of the Salvation Army:

> Whatever may be the actual effects of so eccentric an evangelising agency, there is no reason to doubt that it is adopted in all good faith, as the only way of arresting and securing the adhesion of many who have stood entirely aloof from all religious influences, and have been practically living 'without God in the world' . . . It has undoubtedly had the effect of keeping the primary truths of Religion before the minds of many who were previously indifferent to them.

Referring to the riots, he said:

> All this excitement has long happily subsided. The people of Basingstoke have acquiesced in the wisdom of leaving the Army to its own devices, and the result has been that it has tempered its zeal with discretion, and has ceased to be in any way a serious cause of annoyance.

In November 1889, at the end of John Burgess Soper's term of office, Edward Adams was appointed Mayor of Basingstoke. After receiving the congratulations of the council members, his first act was to appoint Soper as his deputy. He then proposed that a vote of thanks be given to ex-Mayor

John Burgess Soper (Basingstoke & Deane Borough Council, photo Robert Applin)

Soper, which was seconded by Arthur Wallis. Soper told the council that, if he could have spoken for an hour he could not express the feelings he had for the kindness he had received from every member of the council. He could only say that 'this year of good fellowship would be a lasting memory'.[146]

The town, once torn in two by the arrival of the Salvation Army, was now reunited. What a contrast with the situation only eight years earlier, when the council was bitterly divided, and Edward Adams was yelling, 'Down with the Wallises!' and probably winking at the destruction of Soper's Castle; and such a contrast too with William Blatch's mayoralty.

Poor William Blatch had a bad press throughout his term as mayor, and history has not been kind to him either. It was his bad luck that his period as mayor coincided with the Salvation Army's first year in Basingstoke. As the managing director of the town's biggest brewery, he could not be expected to have been very sympathetic to the prohibitionist cause of the Salvation Army. However, if he was sincere in his letters to the Home Office, he tried to tread a careful line between the two diametrically opposite sets of opinion in the town, armed only with the Home Secretary's advice that, if processions are likely to cause a breach of the peace, those processions should be banned. As we have seen, he came down hard on those who disrupted the Salvationists in their place of worship, but less hard on those who disrupted their processions held in defiance of the proclamation.

In July 1881, he told his employees at the brewery that if any of them

---

146   *Hants and Berks Gazette*, 16 November 1889.

John May (Webbers, Basingstoke)

was found to be interfering with the Salvation Army in the future, either in the open-air processions or in their barracks, they would be sacked on the spot, even if this meant sacrificing his most valuable member of staff.

But what about John May, the brewery owner? There are rumours that he, along with the Adams brothers, was one of those pulling the strings behind the Massagainians, and helping to pay their fines and meet their defence costs. Councillor Schofield certainly thought so; and Robert Brown, the Basingstoke historian, recalls interviewing in the 1960s a very elderly man who as a youth at the time, was employed by May's brewery. He stated that there was definite support from May. Moreover, through his great interest in the Cricket Club, John May would have been on very good terms with the three Adams brothers, who were the leading spirits of the Basingstoke Cricket Club Committee. At the time of the riots, May was President of the Cricket Club, Valentine Adams had recently taken over from Edward Adams as Club Treasurer, and Charles Adams was Club Secretary.[147]

It is also clear from the comments he made at the meeting of the Town Council in April 1881 that he had limited sympathy with the Salvation

---

147   Harrison, B. R. S. and P. M. Bichard, *Basingstoke and North Hants Cricket Club 1865–1965* (no publisher noted).

Army parading the streets (and even less sympathy for Richard Wallis). But I can find no smoking gun linking John May to the Massagainians. Nonetheless, I find it very hard to believe that it was only the funds of the Adams family, and what could be gathered by passing round the hat in pubs, that met the full extent of the Massagainians' fines and defence costs.

However, it appears that May left the day to day running of the brewery to William Blatch, while living the life of a country gentleman at Hawkfield; and if he was aware that the Massagainian handbill of 17 March 1881 was being displayed in the windows of his pubs, he did not appear to have raised any objections. When he was Mayor of Basingstoke in 1884, and Captain Coles of the Salvation Army was moving to his next posting after seven months in charge of the Basingstoke corps, May presented him with a cheque for two guineas to aid his work, 'in appreciation of the judicious manner in which Captain Coles had conducted his forces.'[148] He helped to reunite the churches by inviting the nonconformist councillors to St Michael's, and returning the compliment by joining the London Street congregation on two or three occasions.[149] In November 1889, he gave the Salvation Army a brand new brass instrument for its band. He was thanked for the generosity and support that he had consistently shown towards the Army. So as far as John May is concerned, the jury is still out.

Whether it was taking the brewer's silver that meant that the Salvation Army in Basingstoke had 'tempered its zeal with discretion' is uncertain. Certainly a degree of mutual tolerance had set in. The Salvation Army had ceased to annoy the publicans, and the drinkers had ceased to annoy the Salvationists. Familiarity had bred acceptance or, at worst, indifference. And for many people, teetotallers and drinkers alike, the Army was beginning to earn their respect for its social work. By 1898 the Salvation Army nationally was assisting over 18,000 needy people daily.[150]

But what an experience it must have been to have lived in Basingstoke during the extraordinary events of 1881! For many it was a negative experience. In the Council Chamber, in the Magistrates' Court, in the churches, and on the streets, people were bitterly opposed to each other. And for some, it was a time of terror, when stones came crashing through their windows. However, for the neutral majority, it must have been a time of great excitement. There would have been plenty to talk about, and lots of sensational news to read in the *Gazette*.

As for the Massagainians, what fun they must have had: parading round the town, making strange noises with a multitude of unmusical instruments,

---

148 *Hants and Berks Gazette*, 2 August 1884.
149 Manuscript paper, *The Salvation Army Riots*, written by Arthur Hailstone in 1945 for the London Street Congregational Church.
150 Richter, Donald C. *Riotous Victorians* (Ohio University Press, 1981).

and cackling with laughter at the cacophony they were creating; carousing at the Massagainian Banquet; and listening to the satisfying sound of breaking glass. Alas, no memory is left of that happy band of drunkards who roamed the streets 130 years ago. But I like to think that somewhere, in the Basingstoke night, the ghost of Frank Barkham comes reeling through the mists, with his huge brass instrument placed round his shoulders, in search of beer and laughter.

Appendix 1

THE CAST

The information in this appendix is taken mainly from censuses and the *Hants and Berks Gazette.*

THE MASSAGAINIANS

The Adams Family   **Edward** (born 1852), **Charles** (born 1853) and **Valentine** (born 1857) were brewers in 1881, living at the *Shades*, Winchester Street, with their widowed mother, Sarah Ann Adams, who owned the Victoria Brewery. Valentine died in 1896, leaving a widow, Fanny Adams, and four children. When Sarah Ann died later that year, Edward sold the Brewery and other property they owned to Crowley's Alton Brewery. Crowley's paid £8,100 for the brewery, £1,700 for the *Crown*, Winchester Street, £500 for the *Old House at Home*, Reading Road, and £450 for the *Fox* at Ellisfield. According to Arthur Attwood, who as a young man would have spoken to people who were alive during the riots, the Adams brothers used to trundle beer barrels down the narrow Victoria Street to scatter the Salvationists who were praying and singing in Winchester Street,[151] but I can find no contemporary accounts to support this.

Frank Barkham   Frank's given name was Francis Barkham. He was born in 1852, the son of Daniel and Elizabeth who lived in Flaxfield Road. He got married in 1875. In 1881 he was living with his wife, Mary Ann, and his daughter, Ada (born in 1880) at 5 Hadleigh Terrace, Flaxfield Road. He described himself as a painter. Ada died in November 1882 aged two. At the inquest Mary Ann explained that the day before her death Ada had eaten a hearty Sunday lunch of lean pork and cabbage and potatoes. 'She also had a good drink of beer before dinner . . . The child generally had beer on Sundays.' Ada was very ill the following day so Mary Ann gave her some warm stout. Ada died in the afternoon. The jury returned a verdict of 'Death from natural causes through neglect on the part of the mother' because Mary Ann did not send for a doctor, and because of the unorthodox diet. But the coroner said he could not receive that verdict as that would involve a charge of manslaughter, so the jury changed the verdict to 'Death by natural causes'. Frank and Mary Ann had three more daughters, Alice in 1881, Mary in 1884 and Harriet in 1886. Mary Ann died in 1888 aged 33. On the night of the 1891 census, the three girls were staying at Henry Henwood's house. I don't know what happened to the three girls after that. Meanwhile Frank had disappeared to Wantage, where in 1891 he married Christina Garnell, who was 15 years his junior.

---

151   *Basingstoke Gazette*, 13 May 1988.

At the time of the 1911 census, Frank and Christina were living in Wallingford Street, Wantage with their seven children: Lily aged 17, Francis aged 15, Rosina aged 12, Frederick aged 9, Florence aged 7, Arthur aged 4 and Albert who was 10 months old. Frank had kept to his occupation as a house painter. Frank died in 1932 aged 80 and Christina died in 1953. Both are buried together in Chain Hill Municipal Cemetery at Wantage.

Harry Barkham   Harry was Frank's older brother. He was born in 1850. In 1881 he was living at 1 Western Terrace, Flaxfield Road with his widowed mother and his sister. He described himself as a painter. He died in 1890 aged 40.

Joseph Bell   Joseph was born in 1860, the son of an agricultural labourer living in West Street, Overton. In 1881 Joseph was a baker, married to Emily, with a baby daughter, Florence. They were living at 3 Hadleigh Terrace, two doors down from Frank Barkham. In 1891 Joseph and Florence were living in Stoke Newington. Joseph was working as a bus conductor. By 1901 he had become a bus driver and was living in Islington.

Edward Bone   Edward was born in 1857, the son of John and Hannah Bone who kept the *Harrow Inn*, Church Street. In 1881 he was described as a labourer, living with his widowed mother at 6 Cambridge Terrace. I can find no trace of him after that.

James Boon   James was born in 1842 in Wilton, the son of a coal porter. In 1881 James and his wife, Jane, were living in Newtown, and in 1891 at 29 Basing Road. By 1901 Jane had obviously had enough of him – she had moved to North Warnborough, and James was living in the workhouse. James died in 1903.

George Bourne   George was born in 1850. In 1881 he was a bricklayer's labourer, living with his widowed mother at 35 Basing Road. In May 1883 he was charged with sleeping rough in a closet at the back of some cottages in Basing Road. The police were called out at one o'clock in the morning to arrest him because his snoring woke the people living in the neighbourhood. In 1891 he was living in the workhouse.

William Bryant   William was born in North Oakley in about 1848. In 1881 he was described as a railway labourer, living with his wife and two children at 3 Bath Terrace. By 1891 he had moved to Sarisbury, near Titchfield, working as a railway platelayer.

Charles Castle   Charles was born in 1850, the son of a highway labourer living on Basingstoke Common. In 1881 he was a painter, living with his wife, Charlotte, and four children at 5 Darby Terrace, Winchester Road. By 1901 he and Charlotte were living at 79 Lower Brook Street and had eight more children – twelve in all.

Frank Chalk   Frank was born in Salisbury in about 1857. In 1881 he was a mason's labourer lodging with a family at 8 Phoenix Park Terrace. By 1891 he had become a stone mason. He was lodging in Friern Barnet in 1891 and Taplow Common in 1901.

John Clark   John was born in Mapledurwell in 1857, the son of a maltster. In 1881 he was a solicitor's clerk lodging with George Cook and family at 22 Southern Road. When George Cook was arrested for being drunk in Southern Road in 1883, he was described as a publican, the landlord of the *Foresters Arms*.

John Cook   John was born in 1863, the son of a brewer's labourer living in Gashouse Road. In 1881 John was a baker, lodging with a family at 14 Victoria Street. He moved to Nottingham, where he married Emily Fletcher in 1884. Their daughter Kate was born the same year. In 1891 he was a prisoner in Nottingham gaol. While he was in prison, Kate was living in a pub, working as a charlady. In 1901 he was back home with Emily and Kate in Nottingham and working as a labourer.

William Cottrell   William was born in 1857, the son of a drayman. In 1881 he was a baker, living with his parents in Bunnian Place. In 1882 he married Rhoda Foster and they had a daughter, Florence. They were living at 71 Flaxfield Road in 1891. By 1901 they had moved to 30 Sarum Hill. William died in 1939 aged 82.

Thomas Cowdery or **Cowdrey**   Thomas was born in 1853, the son of a cooper. In 1872 he married Elizabeth Stamp. He does not appear on the 1881 census, but Elizabeth is shown as the head of the family, living at 1 Windover Street and working as an agricultural labourer. In 1891 he had rejoined Elizabeth and the children. They were living at 19 Brook Street and Thomas was working as a painter. In 1901 Thomas and Elizabeth and four of their children were living in the workhouse. Thomas died in 1905 aged 52.

William Digweed   William was born in Basingstoke in 1864. In 1881 he was living with his parents at 2 Flaxfield Road and employed as a groom. In 1901 he was married to Stella and working as a coachman for a family in Hampstead.

Charles Doman   Charles was born in 1849, the son of a journeyman carpenter and a straw bonnet maker living in Church Street. By 1861 his family had moved to Flaxfield Road. By 1881 Charles was a house painter, living with his wife, Isobel and four children at 3 Cambridge Terrace. Isobel died in 1890, and in 1891 he was living with five of his children at 7 New Street. Charles died in 1928 aged 79.

Spencer Doman   Spencer was born in 1858, the younger brother of Charles. In 1881 he was a carpenter, living with his parents at 6 Flaxfield Road. In 1901 he was described as a builder and was living in a lodging house in Yorktown, Camberley. In 1905 he married his landlady's daughter. Spencer died in 1941, the last of the Massagainians.

Robert Duke   Robert was a tailor. He was born in Torquay in 1862. In 1881 he was living with his parents in Church Street. By 1891 he and his family had moved to 9 Sarum Hill. In 1901 he was living with his wife and two children in Birmingham. He died in 1915.

Richard Few   Richard was the 14-year-old brother of William Few, the landlord of the *Pear Tree Inn*. William was later the landlord of the *Wheatsheaf*, North Waltham. Richard became a shoemaker and moved to Staffordshire.

Ernest Fitzgerald   Ernest was born Ernest Theodore Fitzgerald in 1856 in Clerkenwell, the son of Elizabeth Fitzgerald. Elizabeth and Ernest and his brothers and sisters moved to Back Lane (now Southern Road) in Basingstoke shortly after his birth, where Elizabeth produced two more children, Percy and Sydney. In 1861 Elizabeth described herself as a tailor's wife. (In 1851 Elizabeth was living with Joseph Fitzgerald in St Edward's Yard, Marylebone. It is not clear whether Joseph accompanied her to Basingstoke.) Young Percy died in 1869. By 1871 Elizabeth was back in London, living in St Giles in the Fields with Sydney and one of Sydney's elder brothers, having left the 14-year-old Ernest in Basingstoke, where he was living at Henry Goring's Eating House in Wote Street and working as an errand boy. In 1881 Ernest was lodging at the *Waggon and Horses* in Reading Road. He described himself as a fishmonger, although the court records gave his occupation as 'hawker'. In 1891 he was living at 33 Hackwood Road with a wife, Harriet, a daughter, Olive, born in 1879, and two sons, Ernest aged 8 and Alfred aged 6. (I don't know what happened to Frances Jones of Windover Street.) In 1881, while Ernest was living at the *Waggon and Horses* and creating havoc in the streets of Basingstoke, Harriet and her illegitimate daughter, Olive, both using her maiden name, Gibbons, were living with Harriet's mother and father in Hackwood Road. In 1901, Ernest and the two boys were lodging at the *Anchor* in London Street. The two Ernests described themselves as fishmongers, while Alfred was a navvy helping to build the Basingstoke and Alton railway. Also lodging at the *Anchor* with Ernest and his sons were 12 other railway navvies and a homeopathic doctor. With the hard working, hard drinking railway navvies, and Ernest Fitzgerald, Saturday nights at the *Anchor* must have been something to behold. In the meantime Harriet and Olive had reverted to her maiden name of Gibbons and were living with Harriet's aunt, the delightfully named Chastity Chase, at 56 Hackwood Road. Ernest died in October 1910 and was buried in the Holy Ghost cemetery. No stone marks his grave.

Mark Harfield   Mark was born in 1864, the son of a hay binder. In 1871 his family was living in Ford's buildings, but by 1881 they had moved to Hackwood Road, next door to the *Horse and Jockey*. Mark was employed as a groom in 1881. He was married in Winchester in 1909 and died in 1931 aged 66.

Daniel Hatton or **Hatten**   Daniel was born in Odiham in 1863. In 1881 he was a carter, living with his parents in Chapel Street. In 1888 he married Clara Rolfe and he and Clara moved to Elbow Corner, where they were living in 1891. His occupation then was a gas worker. At some stage they moved to Lambeth, where their daughter, Bessie was born in 1894. Clara died in Lambeth in 1900 aged 33. Daniel and Bessie moved back to Basingstoke. In 1901 they were lodging with a family called Nash in Potters Lane. Daniel was then employed as a railway carter. It is likely that Daniel died in Fulham in 1908 aged 44.

Henry Henwood   Henry was born in 1863. As a child he lived in Flaxfield Road. His father was a brewery worker. In the 1891 census he was living at 16 Flaxfield Road with his wife, Sarah. He described himself as a bricklayer's labourer. In 1901 he and his wife were living at 21 Gashouse Road. He died in 1908 aged only 44.

Charles Hine aka Hines or Hinds   Charles was born in Basingstoke in 1857. In
1881 he was a bricklayer living in Bunnian Place with his mother and step-father.
He married Annie in 1881 and they had five children. In 1901 they were living at
13 Lower Brook Street. Charles died in 1902 aged only 45.

Elijah Hockley   Elijah was a shoemaker. In 1881 he was aged 47 and living with
his wife, Sarah, next door to the *Lamb* in Hackwood Road. In 1891 he and Sarah
were at 170 May Street, and by 1901 they had moved to Aldershot.

Richard Humphries or Humphrey   In 1881 Richard was lodging with his wife,
Elizabeth, at the *Harrow Inn*. He was aged 40, born in Tunbridge Wells, and gave
his occupation as general labourer. I can find no other record of him.

Joseph Ilsley   There were a number of Joseph Ilsleys living around Basingstoke
in 1881. As Joseph used to get into various scrapes with 18-year-old William
Lambden, he is more likely to be 18-year-old Joseph Ilsley, an agricultural labourer
whose address in 1881 was given simply as 'Near Chinham'. His father was a
woodsman. By 1891 he was working as a farm labourer in Ramsdell and was
married to Jemima. Jemima died in 1919 and Joseph died in 1925 aged 63.

Henry or Harry Jeffrey   Henry was a shoemaker. He was born in 1842, the son
of an agricultural labourer, living in Flaxfield Road. In 1861 he was lodging at the
Queens Head, Mapledurwell, and in 1871 he was lodging at the *Three Post Boys* in
Yorktown, Camberley. By 1881 he had moved back to live with his widowed mother
in Flaxfield Road. He was still living there in 1891. In 1901 he was in lodgings at 40
Church Street. He died in 1908 aged 66.

Alfred Jennings   Alfred was born towards the end of 1856 in Sherborne St
John. By 1861 he and his family had moved to Wote Street, two doors down from
the *Grapes*. He was still living there in 1881 and was employed as a carpenter. In
1883 he married Emily Redgrove and moved to 3 Cambridge Terrace. He and
Emily were still living there in 1901, by which time they had six children.

John Jennings   This is either 16-year-old John Jennings who was a carpenter
living in Sherborne Road, or 20-year-old John Jennings, a bricklayer's labourer,
living at 15 Phoenix Park Terrace.

William Lambden   William was born in 1863. His first home was in Gashouse
Road. In 1881 William was a farm labourer living with his unemployed father and
his laundress mother in Basing Road, next door to the *Engineers Arms*. By 1891
he had moved to West Ham, London, where he was lodging with a family and
working as a meat porter.

Albert Lansley   Albert was born in 1865 in Brown Candover, where his father
was a blacksmith who also kept a beerhouse. By 1881 he had moved with his family
to 1 Mark Lane, next door to the County Police Station. He gave his occupation as
farrier. In 1901 he was living in South Wimbledon. He married in 1905 when he
was 40. He had eight children and died in 1937 in New Malden, Surrey.

Gilbert Lawes   Gilbert was born towards the end of 1842, the son of a butcher
living in Hackwood Road. Gilbert took up his father's profession, but some time

between 1871 and 1881 he became a coal and wood dealer. In 1881 his address was 18 Hackwood Road. By 1891 he had married Elizabeth, a woman half his age, and had moved to 1 Cliddesden Road. By 1901 they had three children. He died in 1926 aged 83.

Seth Lawes   Seth was Gilbert's older brother. In 1882, when George Woodman saw him attacking the Salvation Army, Seth was aged 44, married with two daughters and living in New Road. In 1901, when he was 63, he had swapped his bag of tools for a pen and was employed as a clerk for a plumber and decorator. Seth died in 1904.

Thomas Lloyd   Thomas was born in Mortlake, Surrey in 1863. In 1881 he was in Basingstoke, lodging with a family called Jennings in Chapel Street and working as a labourer. At some stage in the 1880s he married a Basingstoke girl, Sarah, and had a daughter, Amelia, also born in Basingstoke. By 1891, he had moved with Sarah and Amelia to East Molesey, where he was still living and working as a labourer in 1901, by which time Sarah had given him five more children.

James Morris   James was born in Old Basing in 1850, the son of an agricultural labourer. In 1871 he was a private in the Royal Marines. In 1881 he was an agricultural labourer lodging at the *King's Head*, Mapledurwell (now *The Hatch*). He married Sarah Ann Hockley in 1884 and continued working as an agricultural labourer, living on Mapledurwell Common. James and Sarah had 9 children. Some time between 1891 and 1901 the family moved from Mapledurwell to 6 Cliddesden Road, where James was described as a general labourer. He died in 1917 aged 67.

William Phillips (Blacksmith)   William was in his early thirties in 1882. In 1881 he was living in Bedford Place with his wife, Alice, and his two children, William and Edith. By 1901 he was still in Bedford Place, and Alice had given him six more children.

William Phillips (Labourer)   This William was also in his early thirties. He was lodging in Windover Street in 1881. By 1901 he was living at 22 Goat Lane with his wife, Louisa, and two sons and working as a carman. By 1911 he had moved to Down Street, North Warnborough and was working as a miller's carman. By that time he and Louisa had produced four more sons; both Williams had named one of their sons Ernest, whether in honour of Ernest Fitzgerald is not known.

Frank Powell   Frank was born in Upton Grey in 1852. He married a widow, Ann or Hannah Pavey née Marton, in 1874. In 1881 he was a bricklayer, living with his wife and five children at 37 Hackwood Road. By 1891 there were three more children. Frank died in 1907.

Thomas Powell   Thomas was Frank's younger brother, born in Greywell in 1855. He married Alice Jacob in 1876. In 1881 Thomas was a bricklayer and he and Alice were living at 8 Ford's Buildings, Brook Street, with three children. Thomas married Elizabeth Richards in 1894. I don't know what happened to Alice. In 1901 Thomas and Elizabeth were living at 6 Hackwood Road. Thomas died in 1923 aged 68.

Charles Pranknell Charles was born in 1863, the son of an agricultural labourer, living in Gashouse Road, next door but one to William Lambden in 1871. He was also known as Franklin, and he therefore might be the 17-year-old William Franklin, a labourer, living at 23 Victoria Street in 1881.

Charles Purdue Charles was born in Overton in 1862. In 1881 he was a farm labourer, lodging at the *Bell* in London Street. The following year he was lodging at the *Self Defence* pub in Church Street. By 1901 he was married, living with his in-laws in Whitchurch, and working as a labourer in a factory.

Henry Rawlings Henry was born in Baughurst around 1863. In 1881 Henry and his father, Job Rawlings, were ash collectors, living at 4 Windover Street. Henry was fined 5 shillings in July 1881 for driving a horse and cart full of ashes while fast asleep.

George Rose George was born in 1860, the son of a farmer employing 14 men and six boys on 318 acres in Waddesdon, Buckinghamshire. In 1881 he was a seed merchant's foreman lodging with a family at Hollins Grove. In 1882 he was committed to the Quarter Sessions for stealing from his employer, but was acquitted. By 1891 he was lodging with a family in Havant, working as a seed merchant's clerk. He was still there in 1901. While George was causing trouble in Basingstoke, his father was described as a landowner and farmer, living in some style at the impressive Dadbrook House, Cuddington, Buckinghamshire.

Richard Sheppard Richard was born in 1840, the son of a shoemaker in Newton Toney, Wiltshire. In 1871 he was working as a boot maker and lodging in Salisbury. At some stage he moved to Basingstoke, and in 1881 he was a shoemaker, lodging with a family in May Place. He was in lodgings at 21 Potters Lane in 1891. He died in 1904 aged 63.

William Varndell William was born in 1850. In 1881 he was a boot and shoe riveter, living with his widowed mother at 5 Western Terrace, Flaxfield Road. By 1891 he was living at 33 Southern Road with a wife and two children and running a business in Church Lane as a boot and shoe repairer.

CERTAIN OTHER PLAYERS

Henry Barron (Congregational Minister) Henry was born in Hertfordshire in 1849. He was the Minister of the Queen's Road Congregational Church in Portsmouth from 1872 to 1879 when he moved to Basingstoke to become the Minister of the London Street Congregational Church. He remained there until 1886, when he was invited to take charge of the Congregational Church in Batley, Yorkshire. He later moved back south to take a ministry in London. While in Basingstoke, he lived with his family in Essex Road. In 1891 he and his family were living in Deptford, and in 1901 they were living in Wandsworth. He died in Wandsworth in 1902.

John Bird (Newspaper proprietor) John was born in Coleford, Somerset in about 1845, the son of a coal miner. By 1861, when he was 16, he was an apprentice printer, still living with his parents. At some stage he moved to Tiverton, where he met his wife, Emily. According to the *Basingstoke Gazette* website, he bought the local newspaper, the *Tiverton Gazette*. Recognising that Basingstoke was a rapidly growing town at the centre of a vast hinterland and at a strategic position in the rail network, he bought an old stationer's shop in Church Street and converted it into a printing business. The first number of the *Hants and Berks Gazette* was issued on 5 January 1878. In 1881 he and Emily were living above the shop. By 1891 they had moved to Cliddesden.

William Henry Blatch (Mayor 1880–81)   Mayor Blatch was the manager of May's brewery. He lived at the Brewery House with his wife Lydia and their adult children, one of whom was the Head Brewer and another, the Head of the Spirits Department. He died in 1892 aged 71.

Edward Clayton (Salvationist)   Edward was a railway platelayer living in Newtown (now Brookvale) in 1881. He died in February 1884 aged 40, leaving a wife, Frances, and three children. His obituary in the *Hants and Berks Gazette* (16 February 1884) noted that:

> During the long and severe struggles with which the Basingstoke corps in its infancy had to contend, Clayton proved to be as courageous as he was consistent ... Not infrequently during the fierce onslaughts of their opponents was he found to have sustained serious injury, and on more than one occasion he had to go on the sick list as a result. Indeed, it is a question whether his death has not been hastened by the rough treatment he received during that memorable period.

In 1891 Frances and the children were living at 19 Bunnian Place.

William Fenny (Salvationist)   Captain Fenny was born around 1850 in either North Shields or South Shields (he didn't seem to make up his mind on which side of the Tyne he was born). In 1881 he and his wife, Hannah, were living in Darlington. Before joining the Salvation Army, he said he was a signalman on the North-Eastern Railway. At some stage after leaving Basingstoke he was in charge of the Bethnal Green Corps. By 1885 he was a Major in the Salvation Army, working from the Salvation Army Headquarters with General Booth.

Herbert Gear (Salvationist)   Herbert was born in Wiltshire in 1860. In 1881 he was a farm labourer, working for his father at Cheesedown Farm near Deane Gate. By 1891 he had moved to Seaham Harbour, County Durham, where he was running a grocer's shop. In the meantime his father, Francis, had moved to run Bulls Bushes Farm near Oakley.

Daniel Goodall (Salvationist)   Daniel was born in the parish of Wootton St Lawrence (possibly Newfound) in 1842. By 1871 he was married to Jane and working as an agricultural labourer and living in Newfound. By 1881 he and Jane had moved to Basingstoke and were living at 1 The Square, Flaxfield Road. Jane died in either 1882 or 1884. In 1885 Daniel married Mary Ann Franklin. Daniel remained in the Salvation Army until his death in November 1928, aged 86.

George Greenaway (the Hallelujah Auctioneer)   George was born in 1833 in

Highclere. In December 1885 he asked the magistrates to order Elizabeth, his wife, to find sureties to keep the peace, as she had attacked him with knives on numerous occasions and tried to scald him with boiling water.[152] They were still married and living together in 1891.

Mark Hibberd (Superintendent of Police)   Mark was born in Alderholt in Dorset in 1836, the son of a farmer. In 1861 he was a policeman, living in lodgings in Old Basing. By 1871 he was the Superintendent of the Borough Police living above the Police Station in New Street, where he remained until his force was amalgamated with the Hampshire County Police in 1889, when he retired. He moved with his wife and family to 1 Hackwood Road. He died in 1902 aged 67.

George Thomas Jordan (Salvationist)   Captain Jordan was born in 1855 in St Leonards, the son of a chairman. On the night of the census in 1871 he was at sea as a 16-year-old fisherman. In 1881 he was an Assistant Divisional Commander, based in Southampton. At that time he said he had been in the Salvation Army for about five years. Before that he said he worked as a pot boy and beer drawer in a Hastings pub. In 1891 he was based in Worthing.

Richard Moses (Salvationist)   Richard had a most fascinating life. He was born in Falmouth in 1854. In 1871 he was a pedlar, living with his widowed father, who was also a pedlar, in Allens Yard, Market Street, Falmouth, in the heart of the red light district. Of the 22 households in Allen's Yard, 18 were brothels. Both of Richard's next door neighbours were prostitutes. Ten years later, he was the Captain of the Salvation Army in Basingstoke, living with his wife Louisa and young children at 5 Southern Road. He moved to take over the Darlington corps in November 1881. According to Ken Clements, 'Shortly after arriving in Darlington, Captain and Mrs Moses resigned their commissions. It is not known why this happened.'[153] What we do know, is that they moved back to Falmouth, albeit not to the red light district, and Richard's occupation is given as a hawker in the 1891 and 1901 censuses.

Arkas Sapp (Magistrate and deacon at the London Street Congregational Church)   Arkas was born in 1846 in Chichester, the son of a veterinary surgeon. In 1881 he was living with his wife, Sarah Anne and three children above his chemist's shop in the Market Place. He died in October 1886.

John Burgess Soper (Magistrate)   John was born in Padworth, Berks in 1820, the son of Richard Soper. His family moved to Basingstoke in the 1820s where Richard set up shop as a gunmaker and whitesmith in Winchester Street. By 1851 John had his own business in the Market Place as an engineer and gun maker employing two men and one apprentice. In 1861, he was employing ten men and four apprentices. His entry in Kelly's Directory for 1880 described him as an 'engineer & founder, manufacturer of every description of hot water apparatus, pumps &c. Basingstoke ironworks.' He became a town councillor in 1866 and was Mayor in 1889-90. He was responsible for the development of South View and built Hillside in the late 1870s.

---

152   Minutes of the Basingstoke Petty Court, 1883–6
153   Clements, Ken, *Two Feeble Women:The Early History of the Salvation Army in Basingstoke* (no publisher noted, *c.* 1995).

What the Massagainians failed to accomplish, the town council achieved, when, in an act of municipal vandalism, they agreed to the demolition of Hillside in 1989. John died in 1895, aged 74.

Alfred Taplin (Newspaper reporter and organist at the London Street Congregational Church) Alfred lived with his parents in Wote Street. He was a railway clerk, employed by the LSWR initially at Basingstoke Station and then at Waterloo. But a cough, intensified by the London fog, led to a rupture of a blood vessel which forced him to give up his job in London. He studied Pitman's shorthand, and got a job as a reporter on the *Hants and Berks Gazette*. He died of consumption in 1882 aged 23.

James Waldren (Police Sergeant) James was born in Upton Grey, year unknown, but he said he was 42 in 1881. He and his father were gardeners in 1851. He met a tragic end in October 1882. As part of his duties, he used to meet the late night mail train at Basingstoke to see whether any suspect characters were arriving in town. He was standing on the running board of the first carriage, chatting to the mail clerks, when the train set off. He left it too late to jump safely onto the platform. In the words of the *Hants and Berks Gazette*:

> . . . letting go of his hold, he fell under the passing train, and in the same minute was literally cut in twain across the abdomen by the ponderous wheels of the remaining [five] carriages. The porters on the platform . . . arrived at the spot just in time to see the last gasp of the dying man. They were, we should imagine, scarcely prepared for such a ghastly spectacle as then met their gaze. Leaning against the wall of the platform was the trunk of the Sergeant's body, and between the metals rested his legs, which had been so horribly severed.[154]

He left a wife and three young daughters.

The Wallis family Arthur Wallis was a mechanical engineer who ran the business of Wallis and Steevens, famous for its steam engines and road rollers. He lived at Coombehurst with his sons, (Arthur) Herbert, John and Frank, aged 23, 22 and 19, respectively at the time they were engaged in the Battle of Church Square. Richard Wallis was born in 1823. He lived at Eastlands. In earlier censuses he was described as a corn factor, but by 1881 his occupation was described simply as 'Magistrate', which indicates that he was living on his own means. On the night of the 1881 census, Colonel Pepper was staying at Eastlands with Richard. Richard's son, R(ichard) Sterry Wallis, was 25 in 1881. He was an architect and Mayor of Basingstoke in 1903–4 and 1905–6.

George Woodman (Diarist) George was born in 1844, the son of a boot maker living in Victoria Street. In 1881 he was working as an assistant to Arkas Sapp and living above Sapp's shop in the Market Place. In 1885 he set up shop on his own account in Odiham High Street. In later life he wrote a number of articles for the *Hants and Berks Gazette* on life in Victorian Basingstoke. George died in 1932 aged 87. His diaries are kept in the Hampshire Record Office.

---

154 *Hants and Berks Gazette*, 14 October, 1882.

A LIST OF BASINGSTOKE PUBLIC HOUSES IN 1881

Anchor	London Street	*Pear Tree*	Flaxfield Road
Angel	Wote Street	*Pheasant*	Flaxfield Road
Barge	Wote Street	*Plough*	Hackwood Road
Bell	London Street	*Queens Arms*	Bunnian Place
Black Boy	Church Street	*Railway Arms*	Brook Street
Castle	Reading Road	*Red Lion*	London Street
Cattle Market	Southern Road	*Red Lion Tap*	Sydenham Place
Crown	Winchester Street	*Rising Sun*	Chapel Street
Engineers Arms	Basing Road	*Rose*	Brook Street
Feathers	Wote Street	*Rose and Crown*	Church Street
Foresters Arms	Cambridge Terrace	*Royal Exchange*	Wote Street
Fox and Hounds	Wote Street	*Royal Oak*	Bunnian Place
George	London Street	*Royal Oak*	Worting Town's
Goat	Goat Lane		End
Golden Lion	Cliddesden Road	*Self Defence*	Church Street
Grapes	Wote Street	*Shades*	Winchester Street
Half Moon	Chapel Street	*Ship*	Church Street
Hare and Hounds	Flaxfield Road	*Soldiers Return*	Sherborne Road
Harrow	Church Street	*Stag and Hounds*	Winchester Road
Horse and Jockey	Hackwood Road	*Swan*	Wote Street
Jolly Farmer	Bunnian Place	*Three Tuns*	Winchester Street
Junction	Station Hill	*Waggon and*	Reading Road
Lamb	Hackwood Road	*Horses*	
New Inn	Sarum Hill	*Wheatsheaf*	Winchester Road
Old House	Reading Road	*White Hart*	London Road
at Home	(Challis)	*White Hart*	Worting Town's
Old House	Reading Road		End
at Home	(Shepperd)		

There were some others whose names I don't know. When licences were renewed in August 1883, there were 37 alehouses and 17 beerhouses.

INDEX

Illustrations are shown in **bold**; *n = footnote*

Living Lyrics
Poems from Prison

Written By Pastor John Cao

First published in 2021 by
ChinaAid
PO Box 8513
Midland, Texas, 79708

This edition published in Great Britain in 2024 by
Release International. PO Box 54, Orpington,
United Kingdom BR5 4RT
www.releaseinternational.org
Telephone: +00 44 (0)1689 823491

A CIP Catalogue of this book is available
from the British Library

ISBN: 978-1-7375029-0-6 (Paperback)

Layout design by Chandler Book Design
www.chandlerbookdesign.com

Printed in Great Britain by
Short Run Press Ltd.

Contents

Introduction

Blessed are those who are persecuted for righteousness' sake, for theirs is the Kingdom of Heaven. Indeed, my close friend Pastor John Cao is persecuted for his passion to share the good news of Jesus Christ, his love for humanity (especially underprivileged minorities), and his hope for China.

John is a die-hard evangelist. John is always looking for opportunities to share the good news with anyone he meets. He lives out that urgency to share the blessings of the gospel naturally by echoing the calling from the Apostle Paul, '...Woe to me if I do not preach the gospel!' (1 Corinthians 9:16)

I met John around 1993 when he was a researcher in Hong Kong at the China and Church Research Center under China Ministries International (CMI). He travelled to Beijing from Hong Kong where my wife and I had been actively involved with campus ministry. Although he could have chosen to fly between the two cities, he always took a slow train instead. My impression was that every time he got to Beijing he had nearly lost his voice after what he called his 1500-mile-marathon-evangelism journey.

'I need to share the good news with all passengers on the train who have to listen to the gospel because they're riding on the train for hours,' John said with a grin. He obviously looked exhausted but still had a special joyful spirit. God later used John to set up more than 500 'mini-Bible schools' across China. These usually have 12 students with a full-time missionary teacher in one apartment.

John demonstrates his love to others as an 'ambassador for Christ' (2 Corinthians 5:20). He practiced what he preached by helping thousands of individuals in and outside China. For years when I received letters from John, he always had a note in the letter and encouraged me to preserve the colourful special stamps so that he could sell them at an auction to raise funds, so that a number of poor students from China could finish seminary studies in the USA.

When he ministered in Yunnan Province, he found there was no school for the 400,000-strong Shui (which means water) minority group who live in the mountainous areas. He worked with the house church leaders and helped establish the first-ever school for the children in the Shui minority group across southern China.

I last met with John in Hong Kong back in 2016 when we conducted a Christian worldview training event with more than 300 house church leaders. I learned from one of our local coordinators that a Chinese spy showed up and directly warned that John should not speak and would face danger if he did.

However, John could not help but use a few minutes' time of an English-speaking speaker. He shared about revival and the needs among the persecuted Kachin minority group near the Chinese-Burmese border. The Kachin people have long been chased to mountainous areas and have been heavily persecuted by the brutal Burmese military for their Christian faith.

John set up more than a dozen schools with more than 2000 students for the Kachin. These schools are located in remote areas. It usually takes 12 hours by bus before you have to walk a few hours to get to the school. All of the teachers come from Christian households who have faced persecution. John even recruited his own 80-year-old mother. Ironically, John was kidnapped by the Chinese regime and later sentenced to seven years in prison for 'doing good deeds' with his charitable work.

Despite relentless persecution from the Chinese Communist Party regime, John has never lost hope for China and the Chinese people. John firmly believes only the revival of the church through persecution can provide the rich soil for civil society and constitutional democracy. He believes in this vision so much that he purposely chose not to become a naturalized American citizen, even though he could have done so decades ago after marrying his missionary wife Jamie Powell in North Carolina.

I remember when he served as senior pastor of a Chinese church in North Carolina. Instead of being content with his American dream and collecting a good salary, he deliberately asked the church to cut his salary in half so that he could spend half of his time ministering among the poor, needy and the vulnerable across China. John's footprints of hope have already spread into every corner of China. You can see his heart of shining optimism for China from his poems written in his dark prison cell.

I hope this book of poems from John Cao will help you be more zealous for the gospel and love your neighbors more.

I am deeply thankful for my staff and team for making this book possible. I also want to thank those anonymous heroes who helped transmit these letters and poems from John's prison to the United States.

May all the glory go to our Lord and Saviour Jesus Christ into whom John Cao was saved and dedicated every opportunity to, in his decades of ministry.

Rev. Bob Fu, Ph.D.
Founder and President, ChinaAid
Midland, Texas

Foreword

In November 2016 I had the privilege of meeting Mr. John Cao in Hong Kong. I was there to speak at a 'cultural awareness' event, a thinly veiled preaching conference, held at a hotel in the Kowloon region of Hong Kong. When I arrived, John was assigned as my translator and host. I'd never been to the Orient before, but John's kindness and gentleness made my transition there an easy one. His impeccable English and joyous personality made him a joy to be with. We spent the afternoon talking and praying as if we had been friends a long time.

One afternoon, John asked if I would like to learn more about his ministry. Of course, I agreed. He handed me a printed book, all in Mandarin Chinese. I couldn't read a word of it. But then again, I didn't need to. The pictures it contained brought tears to my eyes. John – a shepherd of God's people and pastor of Christ's flock, as only one compelled of the gospel mandate could be – was jeopardizing every aspect of his life to serve the people in the villages of the 'Golden Triangle' of the Yunnan province – the area where China, Myanmar, Laos and Vietnam all come together. A mountainous region, these remote people were isolated by far more than distance. They could neither provide appropriate healthcare for themselves nor could they educate their children. John, with his trusty motorcycle, was serving these people – their physical, mental and emotional needs *as well as* their spiritual needs. He served in impossible conditions and under the most difficult of circumstances. It wasn't that he had no other options. His wife and children were American citizens. John could have left China and gone back to the US. But, with the heart of a pastor and the eyes of a shepherd, John would have no talk of abandoning his people.

5

Near the end of the week John and I shared, I grew concerned about John and his future welfare in such difficult political circumstances. After all, during our week, we had learned there were Chinese watchdogs in our midst of somewhere around 350 pastors. We learned of several pastors who wanted to come but were either prevented from joining us or were warned they should not by governmental officials. John's response was memorable. 'No, Pastor Darin, I'm God's servant. My safety is of little concern. I shall serve where the Lord places me.' As it turned out, this would include even a Chinese prison.

Thus, it was not a surprise when the call came that John had been arrested. Illegal border crossing was the charge. I laughed out loud at that. What was it he was bringing back into China? Medicine. Food. Educational materials. These were to go to the people of the remote villages where John was serving. It was easier to get it in Myanmar and bring it back than it was to go deeper into China. He had done it this way a long time – why now the problem? I believe it was to attempt to silence John and the gospel of Jesus Christ he shared.

For those who reject its truth, the gospel is subversive and dangerous. Its transcendent power and authority render all other authorities to a second strata. As you read these poems, you'll find John understands that perfectly. His allegiance is to Christ and His kingdom first and foremost. His loyalty to Christ and His people – even while in prison – was still on John's lips. Hebrews 13 commands us to remember those in prison as if we ourselves were incarcerated with them. In Matthew 25, in his parable about the sheep and goats, Jesus speaks of remembering those in prison as if Jesus himself were there. When you read these poems, let your heart and mind be focused on Christ who – even now – is caring for John and tending to his needs as John's Great Shepherd. As you read over these poems, remember to pray for John. As you read them, ask the Lord to grant you the same grace, peace and mercy God has given John and that John gave his prison guards. As you read these poems, pray for China and her people. Our God is greater, stronger and wiser than any government decree, prison wall or cell bars.

Praying for Christ's return and remembering John while I wait,

Pastor Darin M. Wood, Ph.D.
First Baptist Church, Midland, Texas

Testimonials

Release International and its supporters have been praying for John Cao and his family ever since we heard of his arrest and subsequent imprisonment, back in 2017. John's dedication to caring for people, meeting their needs and, above all, sharing the gospel with them, are rooted in his own deep faith in the Lord Jesus Christ. Even in prison, despite all the hardships he suffered, his passionate concern was still to share the good news with those around him.

It was while in prison that he first started composing poems. He told colleagues of mine, 'I had never composed a poem before. I had to write in very 'unclear' language, or the police wouldn't have allowed me to send them to my mother. It required wisdom. I started to praise my God and to express my thanks to my Lord and how I was understanding my life in prison and how I can live for Jesus Christ.'

Poetry is not always easy to read – particularly when translated from another language. That is even more the case when the author has to partly disguise his meaning! Nevertheless, this small but profound collection of poems conveys, in gentle and humble ways, the life of a man of faith, living in the crucible of suffering for his Lord.

Paul Robinson
CEO, Release International

John Cao is a living testament to sacrificial love of brother above self and of carrying his cross without shame so others may know the life found in it. He is of those mentioned in the Bible not worthy of this world as they are willing to lose it all for heaven's sake. May his words from a Chinese prison inspire us to be better, to be bolder, and to focus our time on Earth, like him, making an eternal difference.

The Honorable
Congresswoman Vicky Hartzler (R-MO)
Washington, District of Columbia

I first met Pastor John Cao in 2013 in Hong Kong, in a hotel over breakfast. The moment I met him I observed the anointing he had. As he introduced himself, he immediately began talking about what his purpose was here on this Earth, with passion and conviction.

He talked about making disciples in the remote jungles of Burma. He discussed in great detail how they would build schools for children and teach them, from the Bible, how to read and write. He was passionate about showing the love of Christ to these children and giving them hope.

I asked John if he was concerned about the Chinese government and he said, 'God has called me to do this so I can't fear. I am here to make disciples.' Pastor John's energy was contagious from the first time I met him, and you could feel the love from him.

Pastor John would translate and assist with anything you asked him with a servant's heart and an excited smile. He was also an intelligent man. As years passed, he asked me to pray for him as he felt the authorities were tracking him down. Pastor John continued with his warrior's heart building schools and teaching the love of Christ without fear until he was ultimately arrested. He is a true brother in Christ and a hero of the faith.

Pastor Chad Bullard
ChinaAid Board Member
Campus Pastor, Venture Church
Keller, Texas

Our dear brother John Cao is a man of peace in every sense of what that means. Over the years we have served together, in so many different situations, John's presence was always calming. His open smile reflects his satisfaction in the presence of Christ and how John finds that presence to be a constant confirmation of God's provision for him. John's life has been devoted to caring for the downtrodden and persecuted. We can only imagine the influence his life and faith had on those with whom he shared a prison cell.

Mr. Doug Robison
ChinaAid Board Chairman
Executive Chair of The Board, ExL Petroleum LP
Abilene, Texas

From Over the Mighty Water

You can take away my freedom,
but you can't take my prayers.
My prayers have wings
and leap over the towering iron mesh wall.
Many brothers and sisters have heard them.
They fly freely every day
and reach Heaven on the blue sky.
You can impose heavy punishments on me,
but you cannot hold
my spirit and my soul.
Like cheerful yellowbirds,
they raise gentle praises
over the iron gate.
My Saviour must have heard my voice.

You can deprive me of the sunshine, and
Only give me cold leftovers to eat every day,
but you can never extinguish
the brightness
that the Lord placed in my heart.
Greetings from all over the world
warm me.
My passion flutters.

You thought I am alone,
but in your 70 years of persecution,
have you ever seen any Christian walking alone?
You thought your persecution could destroy the church. Fool of you!
Turning onto the book of thousands of years' history,
which page does not reveal
suffering with joy for Christians?
Which page does not show
blood sprinkled
on the narrow path of the thorns?
You thought the walls around me

block my vision
and make me uncertain of the direction.
I never focus on my environment,
but with my eyes.
I look up.
You, like someone blind
ride on the horse,
thinking that everyone
crosses the river
by feeling the stones.

No matter what...
the rod of my Shepherd
comforts my heart.
My Lord helps
and leads me to move forward.

You see me
as an irreconcilable enemy
and thrust me into the meat grinder.
Still, I regard you
as my blood brother,
Not because I am afraid of you,
but because
Jesus loves you.
Therefore, I love you.

Your ancestors stood the sufferings in Kuomintang's prison.
How can I not endure your hard labour?
I really love you,
and long for you to repent.

Like Paul,
I wish that
I myself were cursed
and cut off from Christ
for the sake of my brothers,
for those of my own race.

大水之上

你可以夺走我的自由，却夺不走我的祷告。
我的祷告长有翅膀，飞跃铁网高墙，
众多弟兄姊妹都已听到。
又天天自由飞翔全都抵达蓝天上的天堂。
你可以对我施以重刑，却囚禁不了我的心灵。
它宛如一支欢快的黄鹂，对着铁栅轻轻赞美。
我的救主一定听到了我的声音。
你可以剥夺我的阳光，每天吃的是残羹冰凉，
你却熄灭不了主在我内心安置的明亮。
来自全球的问候，让我温暖，激情飞扬。

你以为我孤苦伶仃，你逼迫基督徒70年可曾见一个踽踽独行？

你以为逼迫能将教会叫停。你真是愚昧呀，
翻开千年历史哪一页不是基督徒将患难喜迎？

哪一页不是基督徒用鲜血洒满荆棘窄径？

你以为四围高墙挡住我视野，方向不定。
我却从不四顾环境，只是双眼向上注目天庭。
你是盲人骑马就以为人人都是摸着石头过津。
我心中自有牧人的杖，自有主搀扶着我前行。
你们视我为不共戴天的仇敌，将我投入绞肉机。

我却视你为骨肉兄弟。

这样说不是因为我怕你。而是因为耶稣爱你，我就爱你。
你的先辈受得了国民党的牢狱，我怎么受不了你的苦役？
我是真爱你，只要你能悔悟，就是我自己被咒诅与基督分离，
我也愿意。

The Mission

Wolves and tigers roar on cliffs,
where Wa mountain people
live in bushes and on perilous peaks.
God called Chinese missionaries
to change the old situation.
Wa children wave
as they
embark on a new journey.

Satan smirks in front of the LORD
until God charges him.
Job enjoys the Spirit
in front of God's judgment seat.

My wish for the rest of my life?
That villages can remain,
and that faithful stewards
can be buried there.

宣教

榛莽人稀尽险峰，断崖时闻虎狼声。
华（众）仆领命改旧貌，佤童挥手启新征。
撒旦主前递控告，约伯台上乘灵风。
余生愿落村长驻，借抔山土留骨忠。

Missing the Mountain Kids

As the bottomless black hole
swallows freedom,
I worry for the children, not myself.
Sporadic good news arrives.
Each school operates well.

惦记山娃

黑洞无底吞自由，不为自己为童忧。
幸有零星喜讯到，学校家家运转周。

The Smuggling

Human traffickers cross borders and break laws.
Day and night,
they smuggle Wa people
to make money from their misery.
As they abuse power, arbitrariness emerges.
Authorities involve righteous people
with no sense of shame.

偷渡

人蛇穿梭践法纲，随到随渡银满盘。
翻手滥权淫威展，迷不知耻义士关。

The Climb

Led by the Spirit,
I climbed the Wa mountains,
for four years.
Never once did I anticipate,
that my own country
would imprison me for seven.
The question fills my mind,
Was the work worth it?
As I count all the lost sheep
who have returned,
God rewards my ambition.

攀登

灵导攀山四春秋，哪知代价七年囚。
撑胸狐疑合算问，细数迷羊壮志酬。

The Lord's Calling

The Lord calls disciples:
'Go to the ends of the earth,
put on armor,
and leave your hometowns—
while it is still day.'
In Wa State, so far away,
mountain people hunger and thirst
to be with God.

The Lord initially used me
to deliver spiritual food.
Now, He calls you
to continue...
where wolves and tigers roar on cliffs.

主嘱

主嘱门徒去极疆，趁光披甲不恋乡。
佤邦路迢民饥渴，我仆你继送灵粮。

Celebrating the Chinese Evangelistic Mission

Forty years under stormy winds,
I fixed my eyes on the stern of the boat
For a decade, inside the prison cell,
being taught by the Lord.
Thousands of servants, led by the Spirit
entered towns and villages.
Being under gunfire,
subjected to painful wounds and being hurt,
facing death,
some shed blood on the path,
yet experienced no fear.

Praying persistently
for dry bones to come alive...
to fill wells
so they would freely flow
in the desolated region.
Often, late night,
dear family members visit my dreams.
Soaking in Jianggang
eventually changes people's faces.

庆祝中国宣教

庆祝中国宣教
四十年强风劲雨
我定睛船尾*
十年牢窗
主教导
万千主仆，圣灵引导
进城入乡
枪林弹雨
经历伤与痛
面对死亡
虽有人在此路上撒鲜血
却未惧怕
时刻祈祷
愿枯骨复活…
井水充足
他们如此便可自由流动
在这荒芜之地
夜半时分常常
亲爱家人入我梦中
坠入酱缸**
终改变人脸

Sounds of Prayers

Travelling thousands of miles
by the wind of the Spirit,
to plant the field,
a young minister
aligns with the Mission
following the narrow trail
winding upward to a higher place.
As I invest my youth
into this remote village,
the sounds of prayers
linger around and encircle
the green mountain peak.

祈祷之声

借圣灵之风
穿越万里
耕种田地
年轻的传道人
遵循使命*
走窄路
蜿蜒登高
当我将青春
留在偏远山村时
声声祈祷
环绕
绿色山巅

In Prison

'Why am I in prison?'
I asked the Lord.
He answered:
'The Jing of flawless life needs to be eliminated.
The narrow mind to be developed.
Due to the shallow understanding of the Word,
these need to be widened by suffering
so that patience will grow.'
When the tribulation strikes,
I look closer to the Lord.
When minor troubles bother my mind,
I welcome the Holy Spirit.
No matter what empty promises
Satan makes to the world,
in the end,
persecuted, Godly people
achieve the victory...
in prison.

狱中

"为何我入狱？"
我问主
他说：
"无瑕人生的欲望要除去
狭隘的心灵要改变
因为对上帝话语的肤浅理解
所以要通过苦难来改变。"
当苦难来临
我定睛主身上
当小事烦扰我心
我迎请圣灵的到来
不论何样虚晃诺言
撒旦向世界承诺
最终
敬虔被逼迫的人们
会成功…
在狱中

A Little Too Long 有点儿长

Seven years of suffering,
seems a little too long.
But, the Holy Spirit
gives me courage to bear.
Taking this opportunity to sharpen
the knife...
to train my heart,
to be ready
to protect the sheep from the
wolves,
even if it seems
a little too long.

七年苦
看似有点长1
但圣灵
赐我勇气去忍耐
借此机会磨
我刀
训我心2
时刻准备好
防狼护羊
尽管看似
有点儿长

Intercession 代祷

Using fingers to count the days,
warriors of intercession
present my name before the throne.
Answers to their earnest prayers
comfort and give me peace.
I can lie down on the green land
and enjoy drinking spring water,
looking forward to the coming day,
celebrating the harvest together.

2019年7月1日
掐指数算日子1
代祷大军
把我名字带到主宝座前
他们敬虔的祈祷被回应
给我安慰给我平安
我躺卧绿草地上
畅饮清泉水
期盼那日到来2
同庆丰收

Keep Myself Pure

He prayed alone
through that long night
in the garden of Gethsemane.
While waiting for the dawn,
as I face this grace by myself,
the joy rushes out.
Persistently watching
and praying
for my people, and
to keep myself pure
at the bottom of Jianggang.

保守我清洁

他独自祈祷
那漫长的夜晚
在客西马尼园
等候黎明时
我独自看见这恩典
喜悦涌流
时刻仰望
祈祷
为我民和
保守我清洁
当深陷于酱缸

Chanting Eagles, Part 1

Flying high, one lone shadow
overlooks thousands of rivers
and mountains below
with sharp eyes detecting movement.
Scanning the landscape below for food,
diving straight down to catch the jackal.
Out of love, stirring up the nest,
to carry the baby eagle,
secured within feathers on the back,
to soar high in the sky.
The owl,
clutching the still scared, rotten rat,
fails to comprehend
the idleness on Yunxiao.

咏鹰 （一）

高飞 只见其影
俯瞰万水千山
慧眼洞悉一切
扫视大地觅食
因爱震动巢穴
背负雏鹰
安稳于背上
遨游长空
猫头鹰
紧握那惊慌腐朽的老鼠
不能理解云霄之上的自由

Standing Pines

Withstanding the sandstorm

in a wasteland without breaking,

resisting the harsh coldness

with dry skin.

Being planted next to a pool of water

to cultivate a garden,

not by human power

but by the anointing of the Spirit.

站松

在不毛之地抵御风暴

而不倒下

用干枯的树皮

抵御严寒

种在溪水旁

滋养花园

不借人的力量

乃借圣灵的恩膏

Love for My Fellows

Love for my fellows
runs deep,
rooted enough for me to suffer.
A multitude of sins
can be fully covered,
cutting off painful nerves.
To face the life in prison
with courage,
connecting with the living spring,
so that I may merrily sing
Solidly memorized,
the stories of Kings
brought a bounty of benefits.

The teachings of prophets,
loaded with rich life lessons,
like the waves of the Red Sea,
the memory card often flashed.
As soon as the prophet
waved the staff,
the dangerous waves calmed.

对同胞的爱

深爱同胞
愿为之受苦
爱能遮掩
一切罪
有勇气
面对狱中生活
活泉在我心
我能欢心唱
谙熟列王记
使我受益多
先知的教导
寓意丰富
如同红海的波涛
存储卡常闪现
先知一挥杖
惊涛便平静

Chanting Eagles, Part 2

Like an eagle in a carved cage
lamenting in mournful sorrow,
shrieking out extended cries,
the only choice
to touch outer surroundings,
while waiting patiently
for the Spirit to secure
the day of release.
When strength renews,
the formerly caged
will mount up with wings soaring
into the heavenly sky.

咏鹰 （二）

如笼中鹰一般
忧伤悲叹
不住哭泣
在耐心等候
圣灵锁定
出狱的日子时
唯一能做的是
触摸周遭事物
再获力量时
囚鹰会展翅上腾

Person with Vision

A vision man in China
abandoned this world to stand for the Lord.
Crucifying the sensuality of the flesh.
Submitting to the Holy Spirit,
to bear precious fruit.

Follow the Lord...
desire to walk the true way
even when persecuted,
heaping burning coals
on the enemy's head.
The only hope for my fellow people?
That they repent.
What resentment could exist
for being in prison?

有异象的人

在中国一个有异象的人
为主放弃了世界
钉死肉体的欲望
顺服圣灵
结出宝贵果子
跟从主…
走正路
即使被逼迫
在敌人的头上
堆炭火
对同胞的唯一愿望？
就是他们悔改
什么愁苦能
在狱中生？

Overflow

His daily prayer
includes thousands of souls.
The cup of blessing
fills the prison cage and overflows.
The physical body,
bounded by prison;
limited to a small range,
suffers bullying for being weak.
In addition to the pain
that sores inflict upon it,
the physical body suffers alone.
Often witnessing servility with surprises,
wondering when that nature will be changed,
the power over this world blinded people,
made their ears deaf.
The army of God still prevails,
overcoming the world,
leading the foreign sheep
to rest on the green meadow.

满溢

他的日常祈祷
牵挂万千灵魂
福杯满溢监狱牢笼
肉身虽被囚狱中
限制在狭小的空间里
因软弱而被欺负
除此之外
伤口疼痛
肉身独自受苦
常惊讶于其奴性
不知何时会变
世界的权势让人们迷失
上帝的精兵在壮大
战胜世界
带领外邦迷羊
安息在青草地上

Chanting Cedars (1)

Violent storms strike throughout centuries,
causing roots to grow deeper,
empowering the tree to mightily stand.
Working together for the day,
they enter the temple as beams,
sheltering souls of the disciples
seeking to find rest.

咏香柏树 （一）

千百年风霜雪雨
使其扎根更深
促其茁壮成长
今天他们一同使用
成为圣殿里的椽
为那些寻求安息之地的门徒的灵魂
遮风挡雨

Chanting Cedars (2)

The old tree with
only a few yellow leaves drifting,
deeply sighed.
Bound and locked in jail,
someday,
the tree will be cut down
to build the school building,
to shelter poor children,
to prepare them to sail.

咏香柏树 （二）

枯树
几叶飘零
深深叹息
囚禁在狱中
某一天
这树将被砍断
建校舍
成为穷孩子们的避难所
预备他们将远航

Hundreds of Thousands

To support me,
hundreds of thousands of friends
clicked my posts.
Help and assistance
relayed from all over the world,
bonding us together;
joining me in the suffering.
Supporting me,
trapped in the desert.
Delivering spring water,
prayers sustain me
to build the plank road,
to climb over the peak
of the dangerous mountain
for freedom.
This new encounter,
the brotherly fellowship
clicks...
to join efforts...,
to proclaim the gospel.

千千万万

为了扶持我
万千朋友点击我的贴子
全世界的帮助
好比接力赛
把我们凝聚在一起
和我一起经历苦难
扶持我
一个深陷沙漠的人
送来泉水
祷告扶持我
修木板路
为自由攀登险峰
新朋友
弟兄般的友谊
点击
出一份力…
传福音

Toughness and Gentleness

Some people say, 'real tough guys also have a gentle side.'
Christians not only need six kinds of toughness,
they need six types of gentleness.

Experiencing suffering, we need tough bones.
Responding to faraway callings, we need tough legs.
Facing and overcoming temptations, we need tough minds.
Hearing defamations, we need tough ears.
Encountering idols, we need tough knees.
In pressing difficulties, we need a tough backbone.

Meeting the poor, we need a gentle heart.
Encountering the truth, we need to have a gentle intellect.
Receiving travellers, we need to have gentle hands.
Helping the weak, we need to use gentle words.
Following the good shepherd, we need to be like a gentle lamb.
Being misunderstood, we need to maintain a gentle mind.

坚强与柔软

有的人说： "真正坚强的人也有柔软的一面。"
基督徒不但有六种坚强，
亦有六种柔软。

经历苦难时，我们需要有钢筋铁骨。
回应遥远的呼召时，我们需要强健的双腿。
面对和克服诱惑时，我们需要坚强的意志。
听到诽谤时，我们需要坚强的耳朵。
遇到偶像时，我们需要坚强的膝盖。
在难以克服的困难中，我们需要坚强的脊梁1。

服侍贫者时，我们需要柔软的心。
遇到真理时，我们需要灵活的智慧。
接待客旅时，我们需要温柔的双手。
帮助弱者时，我们要说温柔的言语。
跟随好牧人，我们需要像柔顺的绵羊。
被人误解时，我们需要保持柔和的心态。

Taste of Treasures

Although moved to Menglian all alone,
many intercessions from the five continents
sent letters.
Though often delayed and difficult to attain,
messages sent with loving care
reached into my heart.
Even in the narrow room,
deep, wide, abounding love.
enveloped me.
Walking alone with book companions,
I enjoy this spiritual rest.
The mystery of treasures
tastes like the nectar of fine flavours.
Laughter overflows into
my whole heart,
Joy outflows.

宝贵的滋味

独自囚于孟连,
五洲代祷
信连连
虽常耽搁且难留,
关爱信息
达我心
虽在陋室中
长阔高深爱,
把我包围
有书伴我独行,
静享属灵安息
这神秘宝贝
味如精致花蜜
欢声笑语
涌入我心田
喜乐涌流

Recognizing Godly Sister, Lin Zhao

Throughout
maniac years of life,
unbearable to remember
the universal lack of integrity,
the foolish mind spoke.
But then,
a meteor lights up the night sky.
Fortunately,
for future generations,
history preserves
a few precious words.

记敬虔的姐妹—林昭

疯狂的岁月里
无法忍受
普世无诚信
愚顽人猖狂
然而
一颗流星划过夜空
很幸运
历史
为后世子孙
保存一些宝贵华语

Mercy to the Poor

Pursuing the one true God
with all my heart and strength.
Giving thanks to
the One Who
died on the Cross,
Who saved me out of the world.
With every step,
obeying the Holy Spirit,
I exercise love.
Loving one another;
showing mercy to the poor.

怜悯贫者

全身心
追求一位真神
向那位死在十架上的
献上感恩
祂救我脱离这世界
每一步
都顺服圣灵
我操练爱
爱彼此
怜悯贫者

Abigail 1

Wise and farsighted,
she stopped a disaster,
sparing innocents
from gruesome deaths.
Recognizing David in his predicament,
she left her household laden with offerings.
Coping with affairs in and out,
She rose to the challenge with a thorough plan.
A woman like Abigail, a gift from God,
joins hands with a loving husband.
~ 1 Samuel 25

亚比该 （一）

有智慧有远见
她阻止了灾祸
让无辜者
免于死亡
在大卫的窘境中尊重大卫
她让自己家物资充足
打理里里外外的一切事务
挑战来临时，她有周详的计划
女子如亚比该，乃是上帝的礼物
与亲爱夫君携手同心
撒母耳上25章

Abigail II

With discerning eyes,
recognizing the hero,
extending a hand
to ease the burden.
On the road,
welcoming the king,
persuading him
with modesty and reason.
Withdrawing the sword,
submitting to God's will,
David revoked his order to kill.
Sharing the aspiration
of good governance,
sustaining the root for future prosperity.

亚比该（二）

慧眼
识英雄
伸手
卸重担
路上
迎君王
谦虚理智
劝说他
勿用刀剑
遵从神旨意
大卫撤回杀戮指令
共享良好治理愿景
为后世繁荣
留住根

Chanting Eagles, Part 2

Like an eagle in a carved cage
lamenting in mournful sorrow,
shrieking out extended cries,
the only choice
to touch outer surroundings,
while waiting patiently
for the Spirit to secure
the day of release.
When strength renews,
the formerly caged
will mount up with wings soaring
into the heavenly sky.

咏鹰 （二）

如笼中鹰一般
忧伤悲叹
不住哭泣
在耐心等候
圣灵锁定
出狱的日子时
唯一能做的是
触摸周遭事物
再获力量时
囚鹰会展翅上腾

Ode to Peter
(John 21: 18-19)

The eerie gloomy prison
appals all.
Yet Peter chooses it
as his burial ground.
The elderly man
offered himself.
The glory
of the reversed crucifixion
never ends.

彼得颂
(约翰福音21：18-19)

阴暗诡异的监狱
让所有人恐怖
然而彼得却把它
当作自己的葬身地
他老人家
献上自己
倒钉十字架的
荣耀
永不止息

Holy Communion

I would go high
and I would go low
for a kindred spirit.
David found many;
Jonah had none.
Bosom friends come
in an endless stream,
to join me
in this Holy Communion.

圣餐

吾将上下而寻求
一个亲人的灵
大卫找到许多
约拿却一个都没有
知心朋友如涓涓溪水般
出现
和我
一同领圣餐

Seeking Truth

As an old man,
I found the only thing
that won't deceive...
words.
Squandered time,
faded in dirt,
creates
this mundane illusion.
I compensate
by dedicating my life
to the great cause.
Disregarding loss or gain,
I seek truth.

寻求真理

作为一个老人
我发现唯一
不会欺骗人的东西…
言语
蹉跎的岁月
消失在泥土中
产生
这单调的幻觉
我用我的生命
来弥补
这伟大的事业
不论得与失
我寻求真理

Child Offers Fish and Loaves

Children,
the most generous,
give away all,
never asking
'Will there be food on tomorrow's table?'
Five unleavened loaves
bring joy.
Two fish blessed
feed thousands and please God.
The hypocrite,
concerned only with the purse.
True believers
thankful for every grain in the bowl.
Sharing the abundance...
better than waiting and demanding.
Open the window
and you will see
the world's broad breadth.

孩童献鱼和饼

孩子
最慷慨
给出所有
不求回报
"明天会有吃的吗？"
五饼
赐喜乐
二鱼被祝福
喂饱万千人让神欢喜
假冒为善人
只顾荷包
真信徒
为碗中每粒米感恩
分享丰盛…
好过等候和命令
打开窗户
你会
看到世界的宽广

The Advent of Christ

Born on a cold night,
the Son of Heaven's eternal king,
a hard life lived.
Pursued by the jealous,
venomous sting,
crowned the globe
with celestial grace.
With pity,
He looked down
from the true cross.

基督将临

生于寒夜
永恒君王之子
一生艰辛
为人所嫉妒
被毒蛇叮咬
却赋予世界
属天平安
带着怜悯
祂在十架上
俯看世人

Ode to Anna the Prophetess (Luke 2:36-38)

She lived as a widow for 80 years,
worshipping
day and night.
Finding happiness
in
fasting and praying.
Benevolent and sweet
her temper.
The holy infant
recognised
her blessed eyes.
She spread
the good news
of redemption,
leaving the earth
with no regrets.
She attained
eternal peace
in the celestial city.

女先知亚拿颂
（路加福音2：36-38）

她寡居80年
昼夜
敬拜
在
禁食和祈祷中
找到快乐
她品性
仁爱甜美
圣婴
认得
她赐福的眼睛
她传播
救赎的
好消息
她毫无遗憾地
离开这个世界
在属天的城市里
获得
永恒的平安

The Same Prayer

Being imprisoned
within iron bars for a year,
not seeing any usual faces
nor hearing any familiar voices.
But unknown saints
increase their love toward me,
growing even stronger.
With joy,
unexpectedly,
receiving a sweet spring of words,
reading each letter
with thankful tears,
we share
the same prayer.

同样的祈祷

囚于铁窗已一年
未见熟悉的脸庞
未闻熟悉的声音
但无名圣徒
愈发关爱我
他们的爱愈发强烈
喜乐中
意外收到清泉般的问候
带着泪水
看完每一封信
我们拥有
同样的祈祷

意外收到清泉般的问候
带着泪水
看完每一封信
我们拥有
同样的祈祷

About Pastor John Cao

Pastor John Cao served as a missionary in Myanmar's Wa State, transforming the lives of more than 2,000 impoverished minority children by building 16 schools and working to fight poverty in the region. Chinese officials knew he repeatedly crossed the border between China and Myanmar because of his work – and allowed him to do so for three years.

However, on March 5, 2017, authorities in China's Yunnan province intercepted Cao and his colleague, Jing Ruxia, and placed them in prison on illegal border crossing charges, despite the fact that they had never had trouble before. Later, they changed Cao's charge to 'organised illegal border crossings.' He was sentenced to seven years in prison in March 2018.

Cao is married to an American citizen, Jamie Powell, and is a legal resident of North Carolina. When faced with the option of obtaining American citizenship, he chose not to, in order to better serve the persecuted Chinese church.

Those observing Cao's case believe his imprisonment did not come from the violation of any border law, but rather arose from China's ongoing campaign to suppress the Chinese church.

About Release International

Release International is a UK-based Christian ministry, called to love and serve persecuted Christians around the world. Founded in 1968 (originally under the name *Christian Mission to the Communist World*), Release International is active in around 30 countries. Through local partners for those countries we prayerfully, pastorally and practically help the families of Christian martyrs, prisoners of faith and their families, Christians suffering oppression and violence, and Christians forced to flee.

Release International's ministry was first inspired by – and continues to be inspired by – the life and witness of Pastor Richard Wurmbrand, who spent 14 years in Communist prisons in Romania, from the late 1940s to mid-1960s. Richard went on to write of his time in prison in the book *Tortured for Christ*, also published by Release International in the UK.

To find out more about our ministry go to our website:
releaseinternational.org.

If you wish to receive regular information or support us in our ministry to persecuted Christians, you can use the removable response form at the back of this UK edition of *Living Lyrics*.

Therefore, if anyone is in
Christ, he is a new creation.
The old has passed away;
behold, the new has come!

2 Corinthians 5:17

若有人在基督里，
他就是新造的人，
旧事已过，都变成新的了。

哥林多后书5:17

John Cao ministering among minority children in Myanmar.

*A Yunnan province prison where John Cao wrote
many poems in this book.*

John Cao speaking at an evangelistic rally.

John Cao (center, in blue) joined the ChinaAid delegation testifying in the European Parliament regarding Chinese house church persecution.

THE LIGHT

TWO OF OUR MINI BIBLE SCHOOL
CLASSES GRADUATING THIS
JANUARY

We sow in tears and reap with songs of joy

2011 has jumped off to a harvest start, with more than 30 students graduating after one year intensive training in the Word of God on January 5th and 8th. Every student read the Bible at least four times besides the classroom teaching. Deborah, one of the students told me that she had read the Bible seven

times in Chinese, New Testament once in English and the Epistles of John once in Greek. This has been a challenging year, but the Lord's grace has upheld all of us through your prayers and support. You may remember that the police raided one of Mini Bible Schools in July 2010, and they detained our trainer

and students for one day and confiscated all of spiritual books, DVD and the computer. The students and the trainer had to run away that night. We fervently prayed for the domino to stop before other schools were raided. And indeed it stopped. All the other schools are fine and safe.

ANOTHER MBS GRADUATION

DEBORAH, AFTER READING THE BIBLE 7
TIMES

2011 ministry update newsletter from John Cao.

John Cao

■■ TO LOVE AND SERVE PERSECUTED CHRISTIANS ■■

PLEASE SEND ME REGULAR INFORMATION:

I am happy for you to communicate with me: ☐ by post ☐ by email ☐ by phone

PLEASE USE BLOCK CAPITALS

Title: Full name*:

Email*:

Mobile: d.o.b: /   /

Address*:

                                    Postcode:

The church I attend is (name of church and town):

Please return to your Release representative, or:
FREEPOST RELEASE INTERNATIONAL
www.releaseinternational.org 01689 823491
info@releaseinternational.org

Reg Charity No 280577 (SC 040456)

DATA PROTECTION ACT (DPA) 2018 AND EU GENERAL DATA PROTECTION REGULATION (GDPR) 2018
All personal data/special categories of personal data are processed in accordance with the DPA 2018 and the GDPR 2018.
Please read our Privacy Statement published on the Release International website for full details.

Do you want to make a regular gift right now?
If so, please use the form overleaf...

YES, I WANT TO PARTNER WITH RELEASE INTERNATIONAL

Please ensure that your address details are also completed overleaf

Instruction to your Bank or Building Society to make regular gifts by Direct Debit

Banks and Building Societies may not accept Direct Debit Instructions for some types of account

PLEASE COMPLETE YOUR NAME AND ADDRESS ON THE PREVIOUS PAGE.
THIS FORM CANNOT BE PROCESSED WITHOUT THEM.

Please pay Release International Direct Debits from the account detailed in this Instruction subject to the safeguards assured by the Direct Debit Guarantee. I understand that this instruction may remain with Release International and, if so, details will be passed electronically to my Bank/Building Society.

Amount: £ ☑ Monthly ☑ Quarterly ☑ Annually

Make each payment on the ☑ 1st or ☑ 15th of the month, beginning on ☐☐ / ☐☐ / ☐☐

These gifts are to be used wherever they are most needed.

Name of account holder

Account number ☐☐☐☐☐☐☐☐ Sort code ☐☐ - ☐☐ - ☐☐

Name of your Bank/Building Society

Date ☐☐ / ☐☐ / ☐☐ Signed

☑ I confirm that I am the account holder and am the only person required to authorise this Direct Debit.

gift aid it

In order to Gift Aid your donation you must tick a box below. I want to Gift Aid my donation:

☑ today ☑ today, and any donations I make in the future or have made in the past 4 years.

Date dd/mm/yyyy **Thank you!**

I am a UK taxpayer and understand that if I pay less Income Tax and/or Capital Gains Tax than the amount of Gift Aid claimed on all my donations in that tax year it is my responsibility to pay any difference. Please notify us if you: • want to cancel this declaration. • change your name or home address • no longer pay sufficient tax on your income and/or capital gains. If you pay Income Tax at the higher or additional rate and want to receive the additional tax relief due to you, you must include all your Gift Aid donations on your Self-Assessment tax return or ask HM Revenue and Customs to adjust your tax code.

The Direct Debit Guarantee • This Guarantee is offered by all banks and building societies that accept instructions to pay Direct Debits. • If there are any changes to the amount, date or frequency of your Direct Debit, Release International will notify you 3 working days in advance of your account being debited or as otherwise agreed. If you request Release International to collect a payment, confirmation of the amount and date will be given to you at the time of the request. • If an error is made in the payment of your Direct Debit, by Release International or your Bank or Building Society, you are entitled to a full and immediate refund of the amount paid from your Bank or Building Society; if you receive a refund you are not entitled to, you must pay it back when Release International asks you to. • You can cancel a Direct Debit at any time by simply contacting your Bank or Building Society. Written confirmation may be required. Please also notify Release International.